The Woman from Hamburg

and

Other True Stories

The Woman from Hamburg

and

Other True Stories

by Hanna Krall

Translated by Madeline G. Levine

Other Press • New York

This publication has been subsidized by Instytut Książ–the ©POLAND Translation Programme

Production Editor: Robert D. Hack
Text design: Kaoru Tamura
This book was set in 11.5 pt AGaramond by Alpha Graphics of Pittsfield, New Hampshire.

10 9 8 7 6 5 4 3 2 1

Library of Congress Cataloging-in-Publication Data

Krall, Hanna
   The woman from Hamburg and other true stories / by Hanna Krall ; translated by Madeline G. Levine.
      p. cm
   ISBN 1-59051-136-0 (hardcover : alk. paper) 1. Holocaust, Jewish
(1939-1945)–Biography. 2. Holocaust, Jewish (1939-1945)–Anecdotes. 3. World War, 1939-1945–Biography. 4. World War, 1939-1945–Anecdotes. 5. Holocaust survivors–Biography. 6. Jews–Biography. I. Levine, Madeline G. II. Title.
   D804.3.K724 2005
   940.53'18'092–dc22

                                                                    2004022648

CONTENTS

Dancing at Someone Else's Wedding

The Woman from Hamburg

1

Their home was far away. They were incredibly sociable; they danced throughout Carnival. They liked horse races and gambled enthusiastically, though (of course) in moderation. They were resourceful and thrifty. He was a master painter; he had worked hard and acquired his own firm and three apprentices. Commonplace jobs, like painting walls, he entrusted to his apprentices; sign painting he reserved for himself, especially if the signs included many letters. He was in love with letters. It was their shape that enchanted him. He could spend hours sketching ever more artistic symbols. Sometimes they were sad because they had no children, but they would soon cheer up—they had each other. All of this was a long time ago.

2

They had turned thirty right before the war broke out.

The war didn't change their life, except that they stopped dancing and new words appeared on their signs. Now, they had orders for warnings. First in Polish: UWAGA! ZAKAZ WJAZDU! Then in Russian: ВНИМАНИЕ! ВЪЕЗД ЗАПРЕЩЁН! Then in German: ACHTUNG! EINTRITT VERBOTEN!

One winter evening, in 1943, he brought home a stranger, a woman.

"This woman is a Jew. We have to help her."

His wife asked if anyone had seen them in the stairwell, and quickly made some sandwiches.

The Jewess was petite, with curly black hair, and although her eyes were blue, she looked very Semitic. They put her in a room with a wardrobe. (Wardrobes and Jews —this is, perhaps, one of the most important symbols of our century. To live in a wardrobe—a human being in a wardrobe. In the middle of the twentieth century. In the heart of Europe.)

The Jewess would go into the wardrobe whenever the doorbell rang, and since her hosts continued to be very sociable, she spent long hours inside it. Fortunately, she was a sensible woman. She never coughed; not even the slightest rustling issued from the wardrobe.

The Jewess was never the first to speak, and she responded to questions with the fewest possible words.

"Yes, I did."

"Attorney."

"In Bełżec."

"We didn't have time to; we got married right before the war."

"They were taken away. I don't know, in Janowska or else in Bełżec."

She did not expect sympathy. On the contrary, she rebuffed it.

"I am alive," she would say. "And I intend to remain alive."

She would watch intently as the wife (whose name was Barbara) ironed or stood beside the stove. Occasionally, she tried to help her, but did so with irritating clumsiness.

She would watch intently as the husband (whose name was Jan) practiced drawing his letters.

Once, she said, "You might practice with something more interesting."

"For example?"

She gave it some thought.

"What about this: 'Once upon a time there lived Elon lanler liron//Elon lanla bibon bon bon . . .'"

This was the first time they had heard the Jewess laugh, and they both looked up.

"What's that?" they asked, surprised, and the woman, animated, continued reciting.

"'Once upon a time there lived Liron elon lanler// Lanlanler lived in the world . . . .' Do you see how many splendid letters it contains? It's by Julian Tuwim, 'An Old French Ballad,'" she added.

"Too many L's," Jan objected. "But I can write OLD FRENCH." And he bent over his sheet of paper.

"Couldn't that Jewess learn to peel potatoes?" his wife asked him that night.

"The Jewess has a name," he replied. "You should refer to her as Regina."

One summer day, the wife came home from shopping. Her husband's jacket was hanging in the anteroom; he had come home from work a little earlier than usual. The door to the Jewess's room was locked.

One autumn day her husband said, "Regina is pregnant."

Barbara put down her knitting needles and smoothed out her work. It was the sleeve of a sweater, or maybe its back.

"Now listen to me," her husband whispered. "I don't want any stupid ideas entering your head. Do you hear me?"

She heard him.

"Because if something should happen . . ."

He bent over his wife's head and whispered straight into her ear.

"If something bad should happen to her, the same thing will happen to you. Do you understand me?"

She nodded—she understood him, and she took up her needles.

A couple of weeks later, she entered the Jewess's room and, not saying a word, removed a small pillow from the bed. She undid the seam on one side and shook out a small amount of down. She sewed ribbons onto two sides. She concealed the pillow under her skirt. She tied the ribbons behind her and, for extra measure, secured them with safety pins, then pulled on a second skirt over the first.

A month later she added some down, and began complaining to her neighbors about her nausea.

Next, she cut a large pillow in half.

As the Jewess's belly grew bigger, she enlarged her pillows and let out her skirts—for the Jewess and for herself.

A trusted midwife attended the birth. Fortunately, labor didn't last long, despite the fact that the Jewess was narrow in the hips and her water had broken the day before.

Barbara took the pillows out from under her skirts and, with the baby in her arms, paid visits to all her neighbors. They kissed her tenderly.

"At last," they said. "It came late, but the good Lord had mercy on you."

Filled with happiness and pride, she thanked them.

On May 29, 1944, Barbara and Jan took the baby and went to the parish church with a couple of friends. ("*Archdiocese of Lwów, Latin rite, the parish of St. Mary Magdalene,*" was inscribed on the certificate signed by Father Szogun and stamped with an oval seal: "*Officium Parochia, Leopoli.*" In the center of the seal was a heart from which emanated the sacred flame.) That evening, they held a modest reception. Because of the curfew, the guests stayed until morning. The Jewess spent the entire night in the wardrobe.

On July 27, 1944, the Russians entered the city.

On July 28th, the Jewess disappeared.

The three of them stayed put: Barbara, Jan, and a three-month-old, blue-eyed baby with fine black curls.

3

They were repatriated to Poland in one of the first transports.

They settled in Częstochowa. (One of Regina's prewar acquaintances had told them that she had distant relatives there.)

As soon as they entered the apartment, Jan dropped his suitcase, laid the child down, and ran out of the house.

The next day, he went out at dawn.

He searched for her for days on end. He wandered the streets, stopped in at offices, inquired about Jewish apartments, approached people who looked Jewish. He gave up his search only after a visit from two men who introduced themselves as Regina's emissaries. They offered a large sum and asked the couple to give the baby back.

"Our daughter is not for sale," Barbara and Jan said, and saw their guests out.

Their daughter was a well-behaved and very pretty little girl.

Her father spoiled her. They went together to sporting events, to the movies, and to cafés. At home, he would talk about how people admired her beauty, especially her hair, which hung down to her waist and was twisted into French curls.

When Helusia was six, packages began to arrive. They were sent from Hamburg; the sender was a woman with a strange, foreign name.

"She's your godmother," Barbara explained. "I don't wish her an easy death, but write her a letter and thank her nicely."

At first, Helusia dictated her letters; later, she wrote them herself.

"Thank you, dear Aunt, I am doing well at school, I am dreaming about a white sweater, maybe angora, but mohair would be better."

In the next package, a white sweater would arrive.

Helusia was ecstatic, but Barbara sighed and said, "If there is a God, she won't have an easy death. Sit down and write a letter. You can mention your First Communion and that white taffeta would come in handy."

Sometimes there were banknotes in the packages. There were never any letters; just once, between two chocolate bars, there was a photograph. It showed a dark-complexioned woman in a black dress, with a long fox fur draped over her shoulder.

"That's a silver fox," Barbara observed. "She's not very poor."

But they didn't get a good look, because Jan took the photograph out of their hands and hid it somewhere.

Helusia didn't like her father's rapturous moods. They were exhausting. She would be studying or playing with her friends, and he'd be sitting there and looking at her. Then he'd take her face between his hands and look again. And then he would start crying.

He stopped drawing artistic letters.

He began drinking.

He cried more and more often, he drank more and more, and then he died. But before he died, a couple of months before his death, Helusia was leaving for France. She was twenty-five years old. A girlfriend had invited her so that Helusia could calm her frazzled nerves after her recent divorce. Helusia came home one day, radiant, holding a passport in her hand. Her father was drunk. He studied the passport and embraced her.

"Stop over in Germany," he said. "Pay a visit to your mother."

"Your godmother," Barbara corrected him.

"Your mother," her father said again.

"My mother is sitting next to me and smoking a cigarette."

"Your mother lives in Hamburg," said her father, and burst into tears.

4

She changed trains in Aachen.

She arrived in Hamburg at seven in the morning. She left her suitcase at the station and purchased a map. She waited in a little square, and at nine she stood in front of the gate of a large house in a quiet, elegant neighborhood. She rang the bell.

"*Wer ist das?*" she was asked from behind the locked door.

"Helusia."

"*Was?*"

"It's Helusia, open up."

The door opened. She saw herself standing there on the threshold: Helusia, but with black hair pinned high on her head, with blue eyes and a too full chin. Helusia, only somehow astonishingly aged.

"Why did you come?" the woman asked.

"To see you."

"Why?"

"I wanted to see my mother."

"Who told you?"

"My father."

A maid brought in tea. They were sitting in the dining room, amid white furniture with tiny painted flowers.

"It's true. I gave birth to you," her mother said.

"I had to. I had to agree to everything.

"I wanted to live.

"I don't want to remember your father.

"I don't want to remember those times.

"I don't want to remember you, either."

Her mother paid no attention to Helusia's sobbing, which was growing louder and louder; she just kept repeating the same few sentences over and over.

"I was afraid.

"I had to live.

"You remind me of my fear.

"I don't want to remember.

"Don't ever come here again."

5

Helusia got married again, to an Austrian—a quiet, rather boring owner of a mountain inn near Innsbruck.

On the anniversary of her father's death, she came back to Poland. She went to the cemetery with her mother. (Barbara was still her mother; she referred to the woman who had given birth to her as "The Woman from Hamburg.")

Over tea, Barbara told her, "When I die, you will find everything in the drawer with the lids."

Helusia bridled at this; then she confessed that she was pregnant and a little afraid of giving birth.

"You have nothing to be afraid of!" Barbara exclaimed. "I was older than you, and even skinnier, and my water broke too early, but I had no trouble giving birth to you."

Helusia was terrified, but Barbara was behaving completely normally.

"Should I notify The Woman from Hamburg when the baby is born?"

"Do as you like. That woman caused me a lot of grief, but do as you like."

Barbara grew pensive. "My God, how happy we were without her! How gay! If it weren't for her, we would have been happy for the rest of our lives."

If it weren't for her, you wouldn't have me, Helusia thought, but she could not say this to her mother, who had given birth to her without any difficulty, despite being old and skinny.

6

In the drawer that Helusia opened after Barbara's funeral, there were two large envelopes among the pot covers. In one of them was a packet of hundred-mark banknotes. In the other was a notebook divided into two columns: "Date" and "Amount." Barbara had set aside and recorded every banknote that had been sent from Hamburg.

Helusia bought long silver-fox furs with the money. She sewed a black dress to go with them, but it turned out that the fox furs were poorly prepared, they shed, and they didn't go with black at all.

7

Several months after her second wedding, she had told her husband about her two mothers. She didn't know German yet. She knew what the word for "wardrobe" was: *Schrank*. "Pillow," *Kissen*, she also knew. "To hide" she found in the dictionary: *verstecken*. "Fear," also in the dictionary: *Angst*.

When she told the story the second time, to her twenty-year-old son, she already knew all the words. Despite this, she was unable to answer several obvious questions: Why didn't Grandma Barbara throw Grandpa out? Why did Grandma Regina run away without you? Does Grandma Regina not love you at all?

"I don't know," she repeated. "How could I know all that?"

"Look in the dictionary," her husband advised her.

8

Twenty-two years after their first conversation, The Woman from Hamburg invited Helusia to visit her for a couple of days. She showed her old photographs. She played Chopin mazurkas for her on the piano. ("The war interrupted my studies in the conservatory," she said with a sigh.) She recited Tuwim. She talked about men. She had had two husbands after the war who adored her. She hadn't had children.

"And what is your husband like?" she asked.

Helusia confessed that her second marriage was falling apart.

"It's because he bought several hotels. He doesn't come home at night. He said that I should make a new life for myself."

She spoke to her not as to "The Woman from Hamburg" but as to her own mother, and The Woman from Hamburg panicked.

"Don't count on me. Everyone has to survive on his own. One has to be able to survive. I was able to, and you must be able to."

"You survived thanks to my parents," Helusia reminded her.

"Thanks to your mother," The Woman from Hamburg corrected her. "That's the truth; thanks to her alone. All she had to do was open the door and walk a couple of meters. The police station was across the street. It's extraordinary that she didn't open the door. I was amazed that she didn't do it. Did she ever say anything about me?"

"She said that if it weren't for you . . ."

"I had to.

"I wanted to live."

The Woman from Hamburg began to tremble. She repeated, louder and louder, faster and faster, the same sentences:

"I was afraid.

"I had to.

"I wanted to.

"Don't come here."

9

"What do you really want?" the lawyer she consulted after her return from Hamburg asked. "Do you want her love or her estate? If it's about love, my office doesn't deal with that. If it's about her estate, the matter is no less difficult. First of all, we have to prove that she is your mother. Do you have witnesses? No? Well then, you see. The testimony of Mrs. Barbara S. should have been recorded. It should have been notarized. Now all that remains is a blood test. Are you determined to sue? So why did you come to a lawyer's office?"

10

"Then which woman's are you, really? And who are you?" her son asked her.

"I am your mother," she said, although, for effect, she ought to say, "I am the one who survived."

But people respond that way only in modern American novels.

Phantom Pain

1

Axel von dem B. can trace his ancestry back to Countess Cosel. It is not entirely clear who fathered her child. According to one version, it was August II the Strong, a Polish king and elector of Saxony. According to another version, it was a Polish Jew, a rabbi who, involved in a conflict with other rabbis, left the country and settled in Germany.

Both versions—the king and the rabbi—have been kept alive in the family of Axel von dem B. for two hundred and twenty-five years.

2

She had luxuriant, raven-black tresses; large eyes that were extraordinarily expressive; skin as white as marble, and a small mouth. That is how Anna Cosel was depicted by memoirists and painters, and by the novelist Józef Ignacy Kraszewski.

August swore to her that she would be queen. He broke his promise, abandoned her a few years later, and ordered that she be imprisoned. Her place of exile was the Stolpen castle. She lived in the castle's tower and remained there (voluntarily, in later years) until her dying day.

The imprisoned countess's favorite reading was Hebrew books. Or so Kraszewski wrote. She surrounded herself with Jews. The rabbinical works were translated for her by her pastor, a scholar of Oriental languages. She paid him generously. At first, she sent him the money through a discreet emissary; later, they would meet and conduct lengthy discussions about the Talmud and the Jewish religion. The pastor's wife put an end to these conversations; she was jealous of the countess, who was still beautiful despite her sixty years.

3

Who was Anna Cosel's Jewish lover?

(He definitely existed. How else can one explain this

peculiar fascination—with Jews, with their religion? He was a fascinating man, that's obvious.)

So: a rabbi—Poland—a conflict with other rabbis—departure for Germany . . .

Jonatan Eibeszic?

He was born in Kraków. He was a sage. He was invited to Hamburg to rein in the angel of death, because women were dying in childbirth. He handed out cards to women inscribed with a strange prayer, with mysterious symbols. He was accused of believing in a false messiah. He appealed to the rabbis in Poland. The Diet of the Four Lands rejected the accusation. Despite the Synod's verdict, many Polish rabbis, including Mojżesz Osterer, the great rabbi of Dubno, pronounced anathema on Jonatan E. and his science.

Salomon Dubno?

He was born in Dubno, from which he drew his surname; he died in Amsterdam. He was married off when he was fourteen years old. He studied in Lwów and in Berlin. He became a tutor for the son of Moses Mendelssohn, the philosopher and theologian (whom many consider the greatest figure of the German Enlightenment after Lessing). Salomon D. persuaded the philosopher to undertake a new translation of the Pentateuch into German. He himself wrote a commentary on the Book of Genesis. When he was in the middle of writing his commentary on the Book of Exodus, Naftali Herc, the grand rabbi of Dubno, came through Berlin. He criticized the friends his fellow countryman was associating with and ordered him to change his milieu. Salomon D. left Berlin without completing his work and set off for Amsterdam.

Jakub Kranc?

He was born in the Wilno region. He was a *magid*, an itinerant preacher. True, he did not quarrel with the rabbis, but nevertheless he left for Germany in order to study and debate with the scholars there. He quit Germany for Dubno. Here he was paid six zlotys a week; later, he was paid two more zlotys and his stove was repaired.

(The Magid of Dubno was asked: "Why is it that a rich man is more willing to give alms to the poor who are blind and lame than to poor sages?" He replied: "Because the rich man has no assurance that he himself will not become lame or go blind, but he knows for certain that he will never be a sage.")

In portraits, all three men have white beards, sad eyes, and a distracted look. Perhaps this is because they had been unwilling to raise their eyes from their open books. But the countess might have met them earlier, when they had black beards and a twinkle in their eyes.

She did not meet either the Magid of Dubno or Salomon Dubno. The former was born shortly before her death, and the latter after she died. But Jonatan Eibeszic was twenty-six years old when she was sent to the tower.

So, could it have been Jonatan? Who, other than he, accused and anathematized, would have dared undertake such a romance? And with a *shiksa*! With the King's discarded favorite.

There is another possibility. Contrary to Axel von dem B.'s family tradition, it was not a rabbi who was their forebear.

It was a merchant. Let's say it was Herszel Izaak. He lived in Dubno and was a fur merchant. He frequented the Leipzig trade fairs. He traveled in the company of his servant, Michał Szmuel. We know nothing else about him, but Dr. Ruta Sakowska, who has translated Yiddish texts for me and helped me discover Countess Cosel's Jewish lover, believes that he was married off when he turned fifteen and that his wife bore him numerous children, became fat, and wore a wig. Should one be surprised, then, that he lost his head over an elegant, beautiful lady? He was handsome, that is clear: blue eyes (they must have looked charming with his black curly hair), a broad smile, dazzlingly white teeth, and a sable fur coat. It is not unlikely that he presented the countess with some sable pelts as well. (Hasn't Dr. Sakowska confused Herszel Izaak with Dmitri Karamazov?)

Well then, the Dubno merchant traveled to Leipzig in Saxony and, as we know from Kraszewski, Jewish merchants were frequent guests in the Saxon castle of Stolpen. They brought goods, newspapers, books; once, they even attempted to help the countess escape from the tower. She succeeded in descending a rope ladder, but the castle guard caught her before she was able to get away.

This happened, this escape attempt supported by Jews,

in 1728. This is what Józef Ignacy Kraszewski wrote in his novel, *Countess Cosel.*

And in that same year of 1728 the merchant Herszel Izaak came from Dubno to the Leipzig Fair. That is what is written down in the history of the city, in the memorial book, *Sefer Zikaron*, published in Tel Aviv. So, could it have been he, Herszel Izaak, with his inseparable servant Michał Szmuel, who organized the headlong escape down a rope ladder?

It doesn't really matter if it was a merchant or a rabbi. What is important is that Axel von dem B. must come from Dubno. Since the Great Scriptwriter arranges and intertwines all these mysterious threads, he knows their future endings, too. For Dubno and for Axel von dem B. as well. So He could not have neglected to provide a common prologue for their eventual common history.

4

Dubno is located in Volhynia, one hundred and ninety meters above sea level, on the Ikwa River, which flows into the Styr. "It looks beautiful from a distance, situated on a hill surrounded by the Ikwa marshes," an old guidebook says. It was a Polish-Jewish town from the beginning. Poles and Jews had to be equally concerned about the condition of the bridges and roads. Jews could bathe in the city bath house on Thursdays and Fridays, and Christians on

Wednesdays and Saturdays. Jewish shops had to be closed on important Christian holy days, but on less important ones they could be open for the poor and for travelers. In 1716 two women were put on trial in Dubno—a young unmarried woman and a widow accused of having converted to the Jewish faith. The young woman was brought before the court straight from her wedding ceremony, along with her Jewish fiancé, the rabbi, and the clerk who wrote out the marriage contract. After sixty blows, the young woman still professed the Jewish religion; after forty more, she returned to Christianity. Both women were sentenced to be burned to death, and the Jews were sentenced to be flogged and to pay a fine in the form of wax for candles for the monasteries, churches, and castle. In 1794 a synagogue was built in Dubno. The lord of the town, Michał Lubomirski, contributed bricks, lime, sand, and his peasant serfs' labor for its construction. During the celebration of the laying of the foundation stone he drank vodka and ate honey cakes with the Jews, after which he expressed the formal wish: "May you pray successfully to the God who created heaven and earth, and in whose hands rests every living being."

Dubno belonged to the Lubomirskis for five generations. Michał, the Lubomirski who helped build the synagogue, was a general and a Mason, and he played the violin. He founded a Masonic lodge in Dubno—the Lodge of the Perfect Mystery of the East. Every year during the annual trade fair he hosted sumptuous balls attended by up to three hundred people a day. Józef, his son, was a card player and a miser. ("He made not a single repair in Dubno because of his miserliness," wrote a chronicler.) Marceli, his grandson, also played cards, but he always lost. Abandoning his home, he went abroad with a French actress. He befriended the Polish poet Cyprian Kamil Norwid, participants in the Hungarian uprising, and French socialists. His discarded wife warned the Russian tsar about a coup attempt that she learned about in a dream. His out-of-wedlock son became an actor in the Paris Odeon. The last owner of Dubno was Józef Lubomirski. He played cards just as passionately as his father and grandfather. He fell into debt. He married a millionairess who was ten years older than him, the widow of a perfume factory owner whom he met through a marriage bureau. Thanks to his marriage he stopped having a dream that had tormented him for thirty years—a dream in which he could not escape from a hotel room because he had no money to pay his bill. He died without issue in 1911. Before he died, he sold Dubno to a Russian princess.

During the two decades between the world wars, Dubno was the provincial capital of Volhynia. It had a population of twelve thousand, the majority of whom were Jews.

5

Axel von dem B. was born on Easter Sunday of 1919. His family home stood on the northern slopes of the Hartz mountains. It had two stories and two wings, and was surrounded by a garden; one hundred meters from the front entrance flowed the Bode River. The locals called it a castle. The family called it a house. They abandoned it in two hours in November 1945, taking only hand luggage. He returned to it for the first time with his daughter and grandsons right before the reunification of Germany. The castle was used as a school of Marxism-Leninism. The director wanted to call the police, because they had driven into the garden through a gate that was actually no longer there. During their second visit, after reunification, the police were not called and they were allowed to go inside.

"Do you still teach Marxism-Leninism?" they asked the director.

"We've switched to English-language classes," the director replied. "But do you know what, Baron? When you've gotten everything back, I'll be glad to lease it from you and convert it into a hotel. What do you say to that?"

His father had managed the estate and studied Far Eastern cultures. He had traveled to Japan and China, and was also interested in the history of civilization. They had had an old gardener, young maids, a faithful valet, a timid governess—all as befits a castle.

Axel von dem B.'s favorite memory was of his governess's conversations with the old valet. Every morning, punctually at eight o'clock, they met on the stairs; the governess was going up to the children, and the valet was going downstairs to Axel's father. The valet was not accustomed to being the first to greet a young lady, so they would pass each other without a word, after which he would stop, turn his head, and say, "Miss Kuntze. Did you say good morning to me, or did you only think that you ought to say it?" This dialogue was repeated day after day, punctually at eight o'clock, for eight or ten years.

Later, Axel and his brother went away to *gymnasium*. Still later, they went to Potsdam to join the army. And then the Second World War erupted, 1939 to 1945.

6

"A corner of Dubno, four synagogues, Friday evening, Jewish men and women by the ruined stones—all fixed in memory. Then evening, herring, I'm sad . . . ," wrote Isaac Babel, who was in Dubno in 1920 with Budenny's army. ". . . pasture, plowed fields, the setting sun. The synagogues are ancient buildings, squat, green and blue."[1]

There were a lot of trees, especially near the Ikwa. People went down to the river for evening strolls. In the summer they went for boat rides outside the city. In the winter ice was chopped out of the river; it lasted until autumn. All year round, water was drawn from the river and carried through the town in horse-drawn water carts. Gas lamps

1. Babel, Isaac. *1920 Diary*. Ed. Carol J. Avins. Trans. H.T. Willets. New Haven: Yale University Press, 2002, p. 33.

were lit at dusk. On market days dust and the smell of horse droppings filled the air.

The scribe Josł had the loveliest penmanship in Jewish Dubno. Young Pinhasowicz wasn't bad either, but Josł was more popular and people brought petitions only to him.

Doctor Abram Grincwajg ("electric-light healing"), who had come straight from Vienna, received patients on Cisowski Street, telephone number 30.

Photographer R. Cukier's business was called "Decadence."

Lejb Silsker had a horse and wagon. He drove to the railroad station, delivered and brought back the mail.

Knives were sharpened by Reb Mejer. He specialized in butcher knives for ritual slaughtering.

The cantor in the great synagogue was Ruben Cypring. He sang beautifully, and also played the clarinet in a wedding band. Eli Striner played the violin, and Mendek Kaczka, formerly a soloist in the Łuck military band in the tsarist army, played the trumpet. Mendek Kaczka's piety was so great that during the four years he served in the army he didn't touch any cooked food, because it wasn't kosher. The Dubno band played throughout the entire region at Jewish, Polish, and Ukrainian weddings.

The amateur theater presented Goldfaden's play about Bar Kochba, the leader of the Jewish uprising against the Romans. Bar Kochba was played by Wolff, the fiancé of Miss Brandla, a seamstress. He was handsome and had a pleasant baritone. The father of Dina, his beloved, was Lajzer, the proprietor of a metal workshop near the well.

Dubno was known for its excellent matzoh, which was thin and exceptionally crisp. In December, right after Hanukkah, they began baking matzoh for sale. Only in the spring, after Purim, did they start baking the matzoh for their own use.

The great merchants traded in hops and timber; hops were sold to Austria, and pine, oak, and fir to Germany.

There were many poor people. Every Friday money was collected for them so that they would not be without fish and challah for the Sabbath.

"A quiet evening in the synagogue, that always has an irresistible effect on me, four synagogues in a row," wrote Babel. "There are no adornments in the building, everything is white and plain to the point of asceticism, everything is fleshless, bloodless, to a grotesque degree, you have to have the soul of a Jew to sense what it means. . . . Can it be that ours is the century in which they perish?"[2]

7

Axel von dem B. crossed the border into Poland on the first day of the war, right behind General Guderian's tanks. On the second day, his friend Heinrich died. That was in

2. Ibid.

Bory Tucholskie. The sun had already set, it was growing dark, and in the darkness he caught sight of the soldiers from Heinrich's platoon running away. They shouted, "The lieutenant's been killed!" and kept on running. The Poles were firing from above, tied by their belts to the crowns of trees. It was not pleasant. They spent the night in the woods.

Axel von dem B. was sitting with his back against a tree; "young Quandt," wounded in the same skirmish, was resting his head on Axel von dem B.'s knees. He was referred to as "young Quandt" to distinguish him from his father, old Quandt, an owner of large textile plants. Young Quandt's mother had died when he was a child, and his father had married a girl named Magda. They hired a private tutor for the summer vacation, a man whose name was Józef Goebbels. When the vacation came to an end, the teacher disappeared together with Magda. For this and perhaps other reasons, young Quandt was not a fan of the Nazis.

Lying with his head on Axel von dem B.'s knees, young Quandt said that he was dying and that those Nazis are all criminals.

"You're not in such bad shape," Axel von dem B. tried to comfort him, but Quandt knew that it was bad and kept repeating that all those Nazi criminals ought to die just like him. "And the sooner the better. The later they die, the more awful will be their end."

Quandt died toward morning, and Axel von dem B. made sure he got a second revolver. He was twenty years old, he had come through his first battle, and he had lost two friends. When they moved on, he held a revolver in each hand and felt quite jaunty.

The commander of his regiment noticed him. "We," he said, "in our family, do not have to give proof of our courage. We *are* courageous," and he took away the revolver that Axel von dem B. was holding in his left hand.

"In our family" meant that Axel von dem B. and the commander of the regiment, von und zu Gilsa, were members of the same family—the great German aristocracy.

Axel von dem B. went through the entire Polish campaign and part of the Russian campaign with this commander. They spent the winter of 1940 in Włocławek. One day, they were informed that the civil administration had designated a quarter into which all the city's Jews would be resettled; the Jews had the right to bring with them only hand baggage.

"What a scandal!" The commander was indignant. "What sort of cretin thinks up such things! First thing tomorrow morning I am going to see Frank in Kraków and tell him everything." (He knew Frank from the Berlin Olympics, when he'd been the commandant of the Olympics village.)

A car was ready for him in the morning, but a moment before his departure his adjutant said, "And what if it wasn't a cretin? What if this is . . . German policy?"

"Do you think it might be?" Von und zu Gilsa hesitated, and then ordered the car returned to the garage. (Later he was named commandant of Dresden. The morning after the Allies' memorable bombardment of the city, he was found dead; his daughter assured people that it was not a suicide.)

They were in Włocławek until spring; in the spring they set out toward the East, and in June 1941, on the morning of the twenty-second, at 3:15 a.m., Axel von dem B. crossed the border into Russia.

He knew that Russia was ruled by Bolsheviks. He knew that there were camps there and that Stalin was a murderer. In a word, he knew that they were fighting against communism and that everything was as it should be.

(Everything was as it should be in connection with Poland, too, especially after Gliwice. No one imagined that the incident in Gliwice had been a German provocation. It was believed that the Poles had lost their nerve; they began it, and it was necessary to respond; everything was as it should be.)

The Russians greeted them with bread and flowers. They, too, believed that the Germans were bringing liberation. Soon, they would be disenchanted; the foreign sonofabitch turned out to be even worse than their home-grown sonofabitch.

That is exactly what Axel von dem B. said during a lecture in Washington, at the Rotary Club, soon after the war. Then one of those present stood up and demonstratively left the hall. Axel von dem B. assumed that this expressed disapproval of his views, but it turned out that it was a protest against his use of the word "sonofabitch." They were among the most refined Washingtonian company, and it was not customary to use such words there.

He marched through Smolensk and as far as Desna; he was wounded six times—in an arm, a leg, and his lungs; each time, he returned to the front from the hospital. In the autumn of 1942 he was in the Ukraine. It was west of the Dniepr, near a river whose name he does not remember, but which flowed into another river, which he also does not remember.

The name of the town was Dubno.

8

People in Jewish Dubno had nicknames. They were used more often than their surnames, and were remembered better. People said, "Ida from Eggs, Beniamin Billy Goat, Beniamin Carpenter, Henia Goose Maid, Red Załman, Black Załman, Crazy Hańcia, Chaim Nouveau Riche, Red Motł, Mechł Beanpole, Jankł Kugel, Nisł Medic, Szołem God Forbid, Motł Water Carrier, Black Basia, Teacher Aba, Wise Icek, Icełe Shotglass, Ester Waitress, Aszer Cymbal Player, Iser Leatherworker . . ."

Iser was definitely a leatherworker, Icełe picked up shotglasses, but Szołem? What event could "God Forbid" be connected with?

Or Crazy Hańcia? Did she have lunatic ideas? Or maybe she was possessed? Maybe, like the mad, wailing Jewish woman from Sochaczew, she would say, "Why do I cry? If you only knew what I know, you would lock up your shops and cry with me."

The people who bore those nicknames are no more.

The people who wrote *The Memory Book* are no more.

There is no one left to ask.

9

Axel von dem B. was a staff officer in Dubno. The regimental commander was Ernst Utsch.

Axel von dem B. had a horse. He would ride out into the countryside. (The area was beautiful: the Ikwa River, an oak and fir forest . . .) Sometimes he rode out in the direction of the old airfield.

One day, during one of his rides, he noticed an enormous, rectangular pit on the airfield. He thought it was probably intended to make it impossible for enemy planes to land. He was surprised: any sort of obstacle laid across the runways would have sufficed. And he turned his horse around.

The next day, the regimental commander was paid a visit by the chief of the civil authority, the Gebietskommissar. After he left, Utsch said that the Gebietskommissar needed soldiers for some sort of action; they were supposed to man a cordon around the entire airfield. Utsch refused; he was not permitted to get involved in civil administration. For a while he and Axel von dem B. pondered what sort of action they were talking about. This was the first time they had heard the word "*Aktion*" in a puzzling, unclear context.

A couple of days later Axel von dem B. was told that something strange was happening at the airfield.

He got on his horse.

He saw the rectangular pit.

In front of the pit stood naked people—men, women, old people, and children.

They were standing in a single file, one behind the other, just as people stand in any normal line, for milk or for bread. The line was about six hundred meters long.

At the edge of the pit, his legs dangling inside it, sat an SS man. He had a machine pistol in his hand. He gave a signal and the line moved forward. The people walked down into the pit on stairs that had been carved into the earth. They lay face down, one beside the other. The SS man fired. A moment later, he signaled and the line moved forward. The people walked down into the pit and lay down on top of the bodies that were already lying there. Shots rang out and the SS man signaled. The line moved forward . . .

It was a warm day, one of those warm, autumn days that occur in October.

The sun was shining.

Naked women were carrying naked infants. Men led children and stumbling old people by the hand. Families embraced each other with their naked arms.

No one screamed, cried, prayed, begged for mercy, or tried to run away. Between the series of shots an ideal silence reigned.

There were eight SS men. One of them did the shooting. The rest were waiting, perhaps for him to get tired.

Axel von dem B. went back home.

The action at the airfield lasted two days; three thousand people were shot.

The evening of the third day Axel von dem B. heard footsteps on the stairs and someone knocked at his door. Someone he knew, a clerk from the regiment's staff, came in.

He said, "I was in a restaurant. The Gebietskommissar is giving a dinner for the SS men from the *Aktion*. The big, fat one is sitting next to him. I heard what he said. He said that they're going from town to town like this. The local authorities prepare everything, the trucks, the cordon, the pit, and then they drive in and kill. He said that he himself has already killed thirty thousand Jews. He said that he was promoted to commander for this . . . Are you listening to me?"

"I'm listening," Axel von dem B. said. "Go to sleep."

The clerk left. Axel von dem B. heard the old wooden stairs creaking under his footsteps.

An hour later the stairs creaked again and the clerk knocked at his door.

"Forgive me if I'm bothering you, but I did a couple of arithmetical calculations. If there are eight of them, and if each one kills thirty thousand people, then they can—over how long a period? three months? four?—they can kill A MILLION. Are you listening to me?"

"Go to sleep," said Axel von dem B.

In November, the Gebietskommissar again gave a dinner, this time on the occasion of All Saints' Day. He invited Ernst Utsch, but the commander declined and sent Axel von dem B.

He was seated next to a woman whose husband was a farmer in the Ukraine. He asked her if she knew about the action. She knew. She also knew that soon there would be no more shooting. There would be trucks that would take care of everything with fumes.

"It's so the methods will be more humanitarian," the woman added.

Axel von dem B. did not ask for whom the methods were to be more humanitarian—the SS or the Jews. He assumed it was for the SS, because the killing tired them out.

He told the regimental commander about everything.

"So, Adolf Hitler has taken away our honor, too," said Ernst Utsch.

Axel von dem B. did not ask what had taken away the regimental commander's honor. He understood that after everything they had learned, they would continue to live, normally, just as they had up till then. They would sleep, eat, digest, and breathe. They would pretend that they don't know. Knowing everything, they would not know.

Three months later Axel von dem B. decided to kill Adolf Hitler.

10

The ghetto in Dubno was organized in April 1942, during the Passover holidays. It was located on Sholem Aleichem Street and adjoining streets alongside the Ikwa River. During the liquidation of the ghetto, people threw themselves into the river, which was deep and fast. Chaja Fajnblit from Rybny Lane, who had been unable to bear children for fourteen years after her wedding and had given birth to her first child during the war, drowned the child and swallowed poison herself. Drs. Ortmanowa and Kagan took poison. Lejzer Wajzbaum hanged himself. Some people tried to hide in the thickets beside the Ikwa, but every so often the Germans set fire to the rushes.

On Yom Kippur, the Jews who were still alive gathered in the house of old Sykuler. The house was next to the Ikwa. The prayers were led by Cantor Pinchas, the *shochet*. After the prayers people came up to him and said, "Reb Pinchas, may we see you in health a year from today."

The remaining Dubno Jews were murdered in October, on Simchat Torah—the Day of Rejoicing in the Torah.

11

Three months later he decided to kill . . .

A decision to kill the Führer of the Reich must take a little time. Especially when one is twenty-three years old. Especially when one is an officer who has sworn loyalty to the Führer.

He felt no hatred. His thinking was cold and simple. Hitler is the incarnation of a myth. The myth has to be destroyed in order to defeat the crime.

He told a friend about his decision. He was Fritz von der Schulenberg. As a university student he had been interested in Marxism; later, he associated with the national socialists; later still, he joined the opposition movement of Claus von Stauffenberg, the future organizer of the assassination attempt of July 1944. (During the trial following upon that attempt, the prosecutor kept addressing him as "criminal" or "scoundrel Schulenberg." Once, when he addressed him as "Count," Schulenberg interrupted him: "Scoundrel Schulenberg, if you please.") He was hanged in August, 1944, a year and a half after his conversation with Axel von dem B. When Axel had told his friend that he was prepared to kill . . .

12

In June 1943 they were in the outskirts of Leningrad, a few kilometers from Tsarskoe Selo and the first front line. It was the season of white nights; one could read until morning without turning on a light. (*"Pishu, chitaiu bez lampady"*—"I write, I read without a lamp"—wrote Alexander Pushkin, a student at the lyceum in Tsarskoe Selo.) It was evening. The sky was the color of skim milk.

They were sitting and drinking coffee in the regimental staff's offices, a wooden villa that served also as the commander's quarters. They had brewed the coffee with hot, Soviet cognac, which they received in their rations along with cigarettes. This coffee was called *café diabolique*. The commander left to inspect the front line. They sat and talked among themselves. It was not a serious conversation—neither about the war nor about politics. Just chatter, really, as would be expected when drinking *café diabolique* at night, when the sky is the color of skim milk.

Suddenly, little Bronsart got up from his chair. He pulled his revolver out of its holster. He aimed at the portrait of Hitler that was hanging on the wall—and fired. His aim was perfect. It is hard to say why he did that; they hadn't been talking about anything serious, after all. Obviously, little Bronsart didn't like the Führer, and that's all.

A deathlike silence ensued, of course. Everyone looked at the Führer with the hole in his head and thought about the same thing: Was the hole in the wooden wall behind the portrait deep, and was everyone in the room a friend?

The silence was broken by Axel von dem B. who asked Richard, the regimental adjutant, if there wasn't a spare portrait somewhere. To which Richard, the younger brother of Heinrich (the one who had died on the second day of the war in Bory Tucholskie), replied that unfortunately there was one portrait per regiment.

The silence filled with anxiety. In the meantime, Richard spoke up.

"We'll think about it later. Before we fully understand what happened, let's each of us do the same thing."

He took out his revolver and aimed at Hitler.

After him, Axel von dem B. fired.

After Axel, Klausing—or maybe von Arnim . . .

What they did with the bullet-riddled portrait, and what was hung on the wall instead, Axel von dem B. could not remember. It was not his problem; it was the duty of Richard, the adjutant, to take care of matters with the regimental commander. Fortunately, he possessed an exceptional diplomatic talent and was suited to smoothing out unsettling affairs.

Bronsart von Schellendorf died near the Neva River one month afterward.

Friedrich Klausing was wounded and sent back to Berlin. Later, he became Stauffenberg's adjutant. He was hanged in July 1944.

Ewald von Kleist survived, but Richard insists that Kleist wasn't with them then.

In any event, three men survived: Axel von dem B., Max von Arnim, who is retired now, and Richard von Weizsaecker, who is the President of Germany.

13

In the autumn of 1943 Fritz von der Schulenberg informed Axel von dem B. that conspirators were looking for an officer to kill Hitler during a presentation of new uniforms. This was about the winter uniforms for the Eastern front. The current uniforms, as had become apparent in the course of battle, were not appropriate for Russian conditions. New models were designed and Axel von dem B. was to model them for Hitler. Himmler and Goering were also to be present at the showing. Since the defeat at Stalingrad the three of them were rarely seen together, so this was an exceptional occasion.

Axel von dem B. was splendidly equipped to act as model.

He knew the Eastern front and he could provide Hitler with essential explanations. He had been decorated with orders and battle crosses. He was tall, handsome, and represented the Nordic type.

Axel von dem B. told Fritz Schulenberg that he agreed.

All the books on the anti-Hitler opposition in the Third Reich mention Axel von dem B.'s agreement. In 1943 "no other German officer, even in opposition circles, was in a position to raise his hand against the Führer." Some men referred to the will of the nation, which continued to be enchanted with Hitler. Others spoke of their Christian principles. Still others, known at one time for their

courage, "were in no position to do something like this."
(They would not have been in a position, to use Richard
von Weizsaecker's words, to abandon the straight and
narrow human path of Christian orthodoxy to seek a road
cutting across the labyrinth.)

After the war, Axel von dem B., a student of law at the
University of Göttingen, lectured to his colleagues. The
Nuremberg trial was in process and his colleagues did not
believe what was written in the newspapers; they thought
it was an error or propaganda. Axel von dem B. told them
about Dubno.

"And you saw this?"

"I did."

"It was Germans who did that?"

"Germans."

The lecture appeared in the university newspaper. It
bore the title, "An Oath and Guilt." Axel von dem B.
explained why he decided to attempt the assassination.
He spoke about the oath he had taken to his leaders.
He said that this oath is an agreement between two free
people in the presence of God, but it was permissible not
to adhere to it if the leader himself breaks it. And the
leaders of the Third Reich had profaned and betrayed the
oath.

Therefore, Axel von dem B. told Fritz Schulenberg that
he agreed.

Richard, as the regimental adjutant, made out a
Marschbefehl for him, a pass to Berlin.

(Fifty years later Richard von Weizsaecker said that Axel von dem B.'s decision was made for him, too. After the action at the airfield none of them, none of the German officers in the Dubno *shtetl*, could say that he DID NOT KNOW. They already knew. And they continued to pass on orders from their leaders to their subordinates. They participated in crimes themselves and drew their soldiers into crimes.

Every day we asked ourselves anew what we should do with all this, Richard von Weizsaecker said fifty years later. Axel gave us the answer. It did not shock or surprise me. We were at the front and every day might be our last. And since that was the case, why shouldn't we decide for ourselves which would be our last day? The death of Axel, should he kill the Führer of the Reich, would have been much more meaningful than a death on the Eastern front.)

Therefore, Richard made out the pass and Axel von dem B. set off for Berlin.

He met up with Stauffenberg.

Claus Stauffenberg, wounded in Africa, had lost his right hand, and his left had only three fingers. His missing eye was covered with a black eye patch. He was decisive, by no means pathetic, and even-tempered.

He asked Axel von dem B. why he wanted to kill Adolf Hitler.

"Do you know what he is doing to the Jews?" Axel von dem B. answered with a question, and then corrected himself. "What WE are doing to the Jews?"

Stauffenberg knew. He then asked if Axel von dem B., as a Protestant, had moral scruples. Catholics understand that it is permitted to kill a tyrant, but Luther wrote in one of his essays . . . Obviously, he had prepared theological arguments for Axel von dem B. and, perhaps, for himself.

"Please think this over one more time," he ended their conversation. "After dinner you will inform me of your decision."

After dinner Axel von dem B. informed Claus Stauffenberg that his decision was final. They turned to discussing the details. The showing of uniforms for the Eastern front would take place at Wolfsschanze, Hitler's quarters in East Prussia. The models would be soldiers who knew nothing. The explosives would be concealed in Axel von dem B.'s uniform. The blast would kill the leaders of the Reich, Axel, and everyone else present.

At the conclusion of this conversation Stauffenberg took a small envelope out of his briefcase.

"This is an order," he said. "You will hand it over to Colonel L. at Central Headquarters. After Hitler's assassination it will be passed on to the armed forces, to all Germans, and to the whole world. You may read it on your way."

Axel von dem B. set about fulfilling his task.

He received the explosives from Colonel L.: three kilograms of mines, one kilogram of dynamite, and one English bomb. It all fit into a small, flat suitcase. The bomb was superb, noiseless. The explosion followed ten minutes after the timing device was set in motion, and the minutes passed in ideal silence. Despite this, Axel von dem B. did not want the English bomb. First of all, he was unfamiliar with it. Second, ten minutes of waiting for his own and others' death was too long. He returned the bomb (Stauffenberg himself used it later, in July 1944) and requested an ordinary hand grenade, which he was familiar with from the front. It exploded after four and a half seconds. True, it made a noise, but one could drown it out easily, if necessary, by coughing. Colonel L. had no grenade at hand, so Axel von dem B. went to Potsdam, to one of his military colleagues. The colleague was a German patriot and a Jewish-German *Mischling.* He had too much Jewish blood to defend the fatherland (this was one of the first Nazi laws: *Mischlings* were not allowed to fight at the front in defense of the fatherland), but he had too little of that blood to be sent to Auschwitz or Terezin. In despair at not fighting at the front in defense of his German fatherland, he begged to be assigned to service in the rear. He was serving in Potsdam. He had grenades. He asked no questions. Axel von dem B. could proceed to Hitler's headquarters.

In the train he removed from his boot top the order that was to be passed on to Germans and the whole world after the assassination.

"The Führer is dead," said the first sentence.

"Several ambitious officers of the SS have murdered him.

"In this situation the army has seized power."

The military sleeping car was traveling east, and Axel von dem B. lay on his bunk, sunk in his reading.

So, Stauffenberg did not intend to tell the Germans the truth. The people still loved Adolf Hitler and it was necessary to pin responsibility for his murder on a "clique" of "ambitious SS."

So we are that weak, Axel von dem B. thought. Even after Stalingrad we are unable to tell the truth. Even we have to begin with lies.

He arrived at the place.

He handed over the envelope with the order.

He headed for the guest barracks. He waited for word of the initiation of the order. The train with the uniforms was en route to Prussia.

He does not know exactly how many days he waited in the barracks, but he does know how many nights. Three nights. He did not sleep. He sat in an armchair and drew up a balance sheet.

When one is twenty-four years old, settling one's accounts, even of one's entire life, does not take long, so he fell asleep on the third night. Toward morning Colonel L. summoned him. The Allies had bombed the train with the freight car that contained the uniforms. The uniforms were burned, the order would not be given. Axel von dem B. was to return immediately to the front in Russia.

Collecting his things, he pondered what to do with the mines and the grenade. He couldn't leave the suitcase in the guest room, and he didn't have time to bury it in the woods. He took it with him to Russia. There, he transferred everything to his soldier's backpack—a canvas one, khaki-colored—and placed it in his officer's locker.

Three months later he was wounded. The wound did not seem serious, but gangrene set in and his foot was amputated. Then his leg was amputated up to the calf. Then up to the knee. Then his entire leg was amputated.

The operation was performed in Berlin, in an SS hospital.

When he awoke from the anesthesia, he noticed a white hospital cabinet. On top of it was a khaki-colored canvas backpack. It was customary at the front to send a wounded officer's belongings to the hospital, so the aforementioned backpack was sent after Axel von dem B. without anyone looking inside it.

On July 17 Friedrich Klausing, Stauffenberg's adjutant, arrived. He said that IT would take place in the very near future.

Axel von dem B. listened attentively.

On the night of July 20 to 21, 1944, he heard Hitler's voice on the radio: "I am addressing you for two reasons. First, so you should hear my voice and be assured that I am safe and well. Second, that you should know about a crime that has no equal in the history of Germany."

Axel von dem B. thought it would be best to destroy his address book. He had no leg and was unable to go to the toilet, so he ate it all night long, page after page.

In the morning the Gestapo arrived. They interrogated him briefly. He had an alibi: he was lying without a leg in the SS hospital. The canvas backpack was on top of the cabinet above the heads of the Gestapo agents. Later, Karl Groeben, a colleague who had a paralyzed arm and had not gone to the front, took it away. He told him about the conspirators, who among them had been hanged, who was sent to concentration camps, and who committed suicide. Colonel L. had managed to escape. Apparently, he had reached the front and sought shelter with the Russians. His colleague finished his tale, took down the backpack with his healthy arm, checked to be sure that it was no longer needed, and promised to throw it into the nearest body of water.

14

"On the outskirts of Dubno there were bungalows with gardens, so there was a lot of greenery surrounding the town. In the spring, an intoxicating aroma of lilac, jasmine, acacia, and night-scented stock, the most alluring of all, wafted through the air. And the river that cut through Dubno was concealed by tall rushes, and was full of fish and water fowl. . . .

"One very cool morning, I don't know if it was autumn or spring, I heard unusual sounds. People were rushing somewhere and I learned that a young Jewish woman and her daughter were swimming in the Ikwa. They hid in the rushes when they noticed that people were gathering and that they could see them. The people were staring at this terrible tragedy and everyone was silent. . . . Someone notified the Germans, and they came and also looked. The woman and her daughter couldn't sit there in the rushes forever; they had to move, because the water was frigid, so they would hide and swim out, hide and swim out, and when they noticed the Germans, they hid again. The Germans took a boat and set out to get them. . . . They were both wearing something white, probably blouses." [From a letter from Antonina H., a former resident of Dubno.]

15

At first Axel von dem B. used a prosthesis, but he felt an unbearable pain in his artificial leg. This phenomenon of sensations in missing limbs is not unknown to medicine. It is called phantom pain. The doctor explained to Axel von dem B. that the source of phantom pain is located in the frontal lobes of the brain, and that it would be possible to perform an operation, called a frontal lobotomy, but the patient refused.

He walks with crutches. He is six foot four. A long leg protrudes from under his jacket. Next to it, between the floor and the jacket, is a long, empty space. The leg that doesn't exist takes up a lot of space. A good deal more than the protruding one, in a dark trouser leg and an elegant moccasin, polished to a shine.

He has ordinary, aluminum crutches that end in pieces of black rubber. Polish veterans, too, use just such crutches; old women in Warsaw, waiting for the tram to Stalowa and Brzeska, lean on similar ones.

He moves slowly. He eyes the surface, taking his time and carefully selecting places that are neither slippery nor steep. He rests his crutches on them and swings his leg. He stops and attentively surveys the surface . . .

He got a law degree. He was a diplomat, a publisher, and a director of exclusive schools.

He has eaten lunch with Theodor Adorno, Golo Mann, and Hannah Arendt.

He spent his vacations with his cousin Claus and Claus's wife, Beatrix, the Dutch queen.

He married an Englishwoman and settled in Switzerland. He visits Germany infrequently. In the fifties he was subpoenaed by the office of the prosecutor. The SS from the airfield in Dubno had been found and the prosecutor asked if Axel von dem B. could identify their faces.

"I don't recognize them," he responded.

"How can that be?" The prosecutor expressed surprise. "Were you a witness to the killing of Jews in the town of Dubno?"

"Yes, I was."

"Did you see the faces of those who did the killing?"

"I did."

"Then why can't you identify them?"

"Because they all had identical faces—like hound dogs," Axel von dem B. explained. "Have you ever seen dogs when they are attacking their prey? Would you be able to distinguish one hound from another?"

Last year, Axel von dem B.'s wife died. He returned to Germany after thirty-five years' absence.

He visited a few people he knew, among them Colonel L. The man who gave him three kilograms of mines and a kilogram of dynamite at Wolfsschanze. After Stauffenberg's assassination attempt he had fled to the Russians. He spent a dozen or so years in an isolation cell in the Lubianka prison and in Siberian camps. After he returned to Germany he settled in Lower Saxony, in a small village house. He received Axel von dem B. politely. Only once did he get upset—when his guest called him Colonel.

"You are standing before a crowned prince," he cried. "Don't you know how one is supposed to address a monarch?"

It became clear that Colonel L. had come back from the Soviet camps as the crowned prince of Prussia. Other than that, he behaved normally.

Axel von dem B. went to live with his children in the old castle. The rooms are dark and cold. Mirrors and paintings in heavy gilded frames hang on the walls. The tapestries depict hunting scenes. The floors creak all night long. It's the soul of an ancestor that makes the creaking noises; he defrauded the regimental treasury, was beheaded, and now roams the hallways, holding his bloody head under his arm. The castle stairs are steep, so Axel von dem B. occupies a little room on the ground floor. It holds a bed, a small table with a coffee cup and an electric coffee pot, a few books, and two bullets.

From time to time a German or foreign historian who is writing yet another book about resistance in the Third Reich comes to see him.

From time to time Richard, the brother of Heinrich von Weizsaecker and former adjutant of their regiment, telephones. They talk about life. Or about Thomas Mann. Or about events that are no longer important or amusing for anyone but them.

Axel von dem B. finds it harder and harder to enter into conversation. He gets depressed. He has been losing weight for no apparent reason. He is bothered by pain that only opiates can relieve. He is not interested in a diagnosis, but he would prefer not to suffer. On the other hand, the thought that this whole joke will soon be over is comforting.

16

Josł the scribe
Young Pinhasowicz
Abram Grincwajg, doctor
R. Cukier, photographer
Lejb Silsker, postman

Reb Majer of the knives
Ruben Cypring, clarinetist
Eli Striner, violinist
Mendek Kaczka, trumpet player
Brandla, seamstress
Wolff, Brandla's fiancé
Lajzer, actor and tinsmith
Ida of the eggs
Beniamin Billy Goat
Beniamin Carpenter
Henia Goose Maid
Red Załman
Black Załman
Crazy Hańcia
Chaim Nouveau Riche
Red Motł
Mechł Beanpole
Jankł Kugel
Nisł Medic
Szołem God Forbid
Motł Water Carrier
Black Basia
Teacher Aba
Icełe Shotglass
Wise Icek
Ester Waitress
Aszer Cymbal Player
Chaja Fajnblit

Ortmanowa, doctor
Lejzer Wajzbaum
Sykuler, owner of the house on the Ikwa
Pinchas the *shochet*, cantor
The woman in a white blouse
The daughter of the woman in a white blouse

And do not remember me in that hour
When God delights you with a great gift . . .
But when my native Ikwa flows
Swollen with tears . . . for those who had
A heart and soul
[. . .]
So long as I have the right
To stand and sing over the graves
Stern, but without anger.

                    Juliusz Słowacki, Beniowski, *Canto VIII (1841)*

Sources: *Dubno, Sefer zikaron* (Tel Aviv, 1966); Kraszewski, Józef Ignacy, *Hrabina Cosel* (Warsaw, 1975); *Encyclopedia Judaica* (Jerusalem, 1971); *Evreiskaia Entsiklopediia* (Petersburg, 1906–1914; translated into Polish by J. Pomianowska, Warsaw, 1990); *Akta Procesu Norymberskiego*, dokument 2992-PS; Finker, Kurt, *Stauffenberg i zamach na Hitlera*, translated into Polish by A. Kaska (Warsaw, 1979); Morawska, Anna, *Chrześcijanin w Trzeciej Rzeszy* (Warsaw, 1970); *Göttinger Universitäts-Zeitung* (Gottingen, 1947); von Weizsaecker, Richard, *Historia Niemiec toczy się dalej*, translated into Polish by Iwona Burszta-Kubiak (Warsaw, 1989); the author's conversation with Richard von Weizsaecker May 15, 1991, in Bad Godesberg; letters of Anna Netyksza from Warsaw and Antonina Hribowska from Czechoslovakia.

Portrait with a Bullet in the Jaw

1

We set out early in the morning.

We were driving east.

Blatt had to be certain that he had returned to the scene of Marcin B.'s crime.

A long time ago Marcin B. had ordered the murder of three people. One of them lies buried in Marcin B.'s barn. Another lies in Marcin B.'s woods. (The barn and the woods are in the village of Przylesie.) The third, who was supposed to die, is Blatt. The bullet intended for him has been lodged in his jaw for fifty years.

Blatt travels here from California. He has returned to Poland over thirty times. Every time he came back, he drove east to the village of Przylesie. He would check to see if Marcin B. was there. Marcin B. never was there and so Blatt would return to California.

2

He always had to drive those same fifty kilometers, so he would either borrow a car or buy a used one. Afterward, it might be stolen; sometimes he smashed it up, or else he left it as a gift. It was usually one of those tiny Fiats. Blatt didn't like to call attention to himself.

("You can call me Tomek," he said the first day. "Or Tojwełe, as I was called when I was a child. Or Thomas, as it says in my American passport." I continued to think of him as Blatt, despite so many possibilities.)

We were driving east.

The sun was shining in through the windshield. In the brilliant light Blatt's temples were completely gray, even though he had dark-red hair on his head. I asked him if he dyed his hair. He explained that it's not a dye, but a special liquid. In the morning, while combing his hair, he pours a few drops on the comb.

"American," I guessed. He nodded; the latest invention.

Blatt was not tall, but he was thickset and strong. It was easy to imagine him in front of a mirror: a short neck, broad torso, an undershirt and a bottle of the latest American anti-graying liquid. But this image should not evoke an ironic smile. Blatt's strength today is the same as the strength that commanded him to survive. Blatt's strength should be treated seriously. Just like his love affairs, all of them with blondes. His Jewish postwar love had to be a blonde. Only an Aryan woman with light blond hair could personify a refined and safe world.

Blatt's cousin, Dawid Klein, lived in Berlin before the war. He survived Auschwitz and returned to Berlin. He found new tenants living in his apartment.

"There's no need to get upset," they said. "Everything is where you left it."

Indeed, he found absolutely everything exactly where he had left it before the war.

He married their blond daughter. She was the war widow of an SS officer. Blatt's cousin raised their son. When his wife fell in love with a younger man, Blatt's cousin died of a heart attack. (I phoned their daughter in Berlin. Her husband picked up the phone. I said that I wanted to talk about Dawid Klein, who was an Auschwitz survivor. I heard him call out to Dawid Klein's daughter, "Was your father an Auschwitz survivor?")

Staszek Szmajzner, a jeweler from Sobibor, emigrated to Rio. True, he did not marry an Aryan woman; instead, he married a Miss Brazil. They got divorced. Staszek went to the jungle and wrote a book about Sobibor. When he finished it, he died of a heart attack.

Hersz Cukierman, the son of a cook from Sobibor, went to Germany. His Aryan wife left him and Cukierman hanged himself.

And so forth.

Blatt is still writing his book.

We were traveling east.

Blatt wanted to ascertain if Marcin B. had returned to the village of Przylesie.

3

We passed former Jewish towns: Garwolin, Łopiennik, Krasnystaw, Izbica. The stucco on them was yellowed, with dirty streaks. The wooden, one-story bungalows were sinking into the ground. We wondered if anyone lived in them. Probably yes, because there were pots of pelargonia in the windows, wrapped in crimped white tissue paper. Wads of cotton were spread out on some of the windowsills. Silvery "angel hair," left there, no doubt, since Christmas, sparkled on the cotton. Men wearing gray quilted jackets were drinking beer outside the entryway. Apparently there were no unoccupied seats inside. Chunks of wall stuck up in empty lots among the houses. Grass was growing out of the smashed bricks. The little towns had flabby faces;

they were deprived of muscle, deformed—either by exhaustion or by fear.

In Izbica, Blatt wanted to show me a couple of things. We began with Stokowa Street. Generations of Blatts had lived there, including Aunt Marie Rojtensztajn, who heard everything through the wall. "Tojwełe," she would say, "admit it, your father gives you nonkosher food to eat. You'll go to hell, Tojwełe."

He was so terrified of hell that he ran a fever.

"You're only eight years old," his aunt comforted him. "After you are bar mitzvah, God will forgive you everything."

He calculated that he could sin for five more years. Unfortunately, the war began before his bar mitzvah; God forgave him nothing.

We looked around the market square. Idełe used to stand in the center, banging on a drum. He read out the declarations that the authorities posted. He banged his drum for the last time in September 1939, and announced that they were to cover their windows to protect them from bombs. He died in Bełżec.

Itinerant musicians used to play in the market square; they sold the words to the latest hit songs for five groschen. Tojwełe bought "Madagascar"—"Hey, Madagascar, steamy land, black, Africa . . ."

The fanciest house on the market square belonged to Juda Pomp, a dealer in sheet metal. He installed a flush toilet in his home, the first in Izbica. Everyone came to check it out; an inside toilet, and it doesn't stink!

We finally finished with the market square and moved on to the side streets. We came upon the house of crazy Ryfka "What Time Is It?" "Ryfka, what time is it?" the children called out to her. She would answer precisely and she never made a mistake. An old Jew, ugly and rich, arrived from America. He looked Ryfka over. He learned that she was the daughter of a deceased rabbi. He told her to comb her hair and they got married. The inhabitants of Izbica had to admit that after the wedding Ryfka turned out to be a nice-looking woman without a trace of madness. She bore a child. They all died in Sobibor.

Nearby lived a Captain Dr. Lind. What was his first name? What brand of car he owned is known: an Opel. But then, it was the only car in Izbica. On the first of September 1939 the doctor's wife cleaned the house, changed the linens and—what Tojwełe's mother, Fajga Blatt, admired even more—placed a clean tablecloth on the table. Then the doctor donned his uniform and they got into the Opel. The doctor died at Katyń; where his wife died is not known.

Flajszman the tailor sewed clothes for Tojwełe and his brother. The Flajszmans had a single room and nine children. They knocked together boards to make a bed large enough for all of them. A sewing machine stood under the window and a table stood in the middle of the room. But they ate at the table only on Shabbos; on weekdays, it served as an ironing board. The Flajszmans and their nine children died in Bełżec.

Shochet Wajnsztajn, the ritual slaughterer. He studied Talmud all day long, and Mrs. Wajnsztajn supported their household with ice cream and soda water. She made the ice cream in a wooden barrel placed inside a container filled with salt. The sanitarian did not permit the use of cheap, unwashed salt in food preparation, and Mrs. Wajnsztajn could not afford the more expensive salt, so her sons Symcha and Jankiel kept a lookout at the door for the police. They died in Bełżec.

The house of Mrs. Bunszpan; her surname has to be changed for obvious reasons. She had a hardware store. She had a fair-skinned daughter and a dark little boy. She told him to stay inside the house while she and her daughter went to the train station. The boy ran after them. He tried to get on the train with his mother, but Mrs. Bunszpan pushed him away.

"Go away," she said, "Be a good boy." He was a good boy. He died in Bełżec. Mrs. Bunszpan and her daughter survived the war.

"I have learned," said Blatt, "that no one knows himself thoroughly."

Rojza Nasybirska's brewery. She ran away from a transport. She entered the first house she came to. There were people sitting at the table, reading the Bible. They were Jehovah's Witnesses. They decided that Rojza was a sign sent by God Himself. They gave her a Bible and told her to convert others. She waited out the end of the war in peace. It never entered anyone's mind that it was a Jewish woman who was walking from village to village, converting people. After the war, she wanted to keep on converting people out of gratitude, but her cousin came and took her to the States.

Hersz Goldberg's lumberyard. Cut lumber was stacked neatly everywhere. When the first star appeared in the sky on Saturday and Shabbos came to an end, people drank wine from a common goblet and said to each other, "*Git vokh*, have a good week." That was a signal for the young folk; the boys would head out with their girlfriends to Goldberg's lumber. Their younger siblings followed them to see what went on in the evenings on top of the lumber. Hersz Goldberg died in Bełżec.

A shack near the Jewish cemetery. Jankiel Blatt, Tojwełe's father's brother, lived there. He had two children and no job; he was a communist. When the Russians took over in September 1939, Uncle Jankiel greeted them enthusiastically. "Now there will be jobs," he kept repeating, "now there will be justice."

The communists put on red armbands and showed the Russians who the Polish and Jewish bourgeoisie were, and also pointed out the soldiers returning from the September campaign. Among those arrested was Juda Pomp, the sheet metal merchant and owner of the house with the toilet. Tojwełe's father, a former Legionnaire, threw Uncle Jankiel out of the house, shouting that he wasn't to show himself to him ever again. Two weeks later the Russians withdrew. The Germans occupied the town. The communist Jankiel Blatt died and so did Juda Pomp, the class enemy. He would have had a much better chance in Siberia than in Sobibor, but the Russians, alas, hadn't had enough time to send the Izbica bourgeoisie to the gulag.

Blatt talked and talked. Izbica had had three thousand Jews, and he was still on the first hundred. Now he was getting ready to visit Małka Lerner, the butcher's daughter; we were passing their house. Małka—erect, tall, dark, first among the well-to-do girls—opened the door wearing a sky-blue bathrobe. Offering him cake, she bent over slightly, revealing her décolleté. Not by accident, and not with embarrassment, but with obvious pride. She was twelve years old and she already had breasts. The cakes were sprinkled with poppy seed. Such cakes were carried around to one's neighbors for Purim, on a plate covered with a white, hem-stitched napkin. Małka carried them round to the wealthy girls, and Estera, who was shorter, petite, with blond hair, took them to the poor girls. She wasn't strikingly beautiful, but she would have been better looking in old age than Małka, Blatt admitted somewhat reluctantly. He seemed to be pondering whether he was being disloyal to Małka. Estera would have been thinner and with a better figure, but she did not grow old. Józek Bressler, the dentist's son, told him in the camp that he had traveled in the same freight car with Estera and Małka. "Look," Małka had said, "I'm fifteen, I've never made love to a boy and now I'll never know what that's like." They both died. Józek Bressler ran away with everyone, but he was blown apart by a land mine.

Finally, the last house, Grandma Chana Sura's; she was a Klein by birth, the aunt of the Berlin cousin. She wore a wig. She didn't visit the Blatts because Tojwełe's father, Leon Blatt, who had been given a concession to sell vodka and wines as a reward for his service in the Polish Legion, ate nonkosher food, did not observe the Sabbath, and had been excommunicated by the rabbi. Kurt Engels, the Gestapo chief, personally placed a crown of thorns made from barbed wire on his head and hung a sign around his neck: "I am Christ. Izbica is the new capital of the Jews." He roared with laughter as Leon Blatt walked through Izbica wearing his crown. Grandma Chana Sura, Leon Blatt, his wife Fajga, and Herszel, Tojwełe's younger brother, died in Sobibor.

And now it's really the last house. The remains of a house, with remnants of a wall—Mosze Blank's tannery. After the first deportation people took shelter in it. They felt safe; they said, come what may, the Germans will always need skins. They died in Sobibor. The owner's sons survived. The older one, Jankiel, was a student at the famous Lublin yeshiva before the war. He had his Talmud in his hiding place near Kurów and continued his studies by the light of a kerosene lamp. He barely noticed when the war ended. The younger boy, Hersz, went into busi-

ness after the war. He was murdered in Lublin, by unknown assailants, on Kowalska Street.

We turned to the southeast.

4

The rebellion in Sobibor, the largest uprising in the concentration camps, took place on October 14, 1943. It was
led by Aleksander Peczerski, a Red Army officer and a
prisoner of war. Following the uprising, the Germans liq-
uidated the camp.

In Sobibor there were workshops producing things for
the Germans. At three thirty in the afternoon the tailors
informed one of the SS that his new uniform was ready to
be measured. The SS man undressed and set aside his belt
with his revolver. The tailors killed him with an ax and
scissors. They placed his body in a closet, covered the blood
on the floor with rags, and invited the next SS man to come
in. At the same time, the shoemakers were announcing that
boots were ready, and the carpenters, that there was beautiful furniture to inspect. Almost all the SS who were on
duty died. This played out in silence and lasted an hour
and a half. At five o'clock several hundred prisoners formed
a column. Peczerski shouted in Russian, *"Za rodinu, za
Stalina, vpered!"*—"For the Fatherland, for Stalin, forward!" The people ran toward the woods. Many of them

died immediately in the minefield. Tojwełe's jacket got caught on the fence and for a moment he couldn't extricate himself. When he started running again the field was already free of mines. The Americans made a television film called *Escape from Sobibor*. Blatt was a consultant. He was played by a young American actor. The actor got caught on the fence, just like Tojwełe, and, as the script dictated, he was unable to extricate himself. It seemed to Blatt that this was taking too long. He was terrified. Time was passing, and he was not escaping from Sobibor. When the actor set off across the field, Blatt started running with him. The shot had long since been completed, but Blatt kept running. They found him several hours later, covered with scratches, his eyeglasses broken, hiding in the woods.

Karl Frenzel was an SS man who survived. He had no desire for a new uniform, boots, or furniture. After the war he was given seven life sentences. In 1984 he won the right to a new trial. The trial took place in the Hague. Blatt was a witness for the prosecution. He remembered Frenzel perfectly. When his parents, his brother, and he emerged from the freight train in Sobibor, Frenzel was conducting the selection personally and sending people to the gas chamber. A day earlier, when they were still at home, Tojwełe had drunk up all the milk that was supposed to last for several days. His mother had said, "Don't drink so much; leave some for tomorrow." The day after that they were standing on the ramp in Sobibor. "You see," he told his mother, "and you wanted to save some milk for today." Those were the last words he said to his mother. He can still hear them fifty years later. He had intended to discuss this with a psychiatrist, but it's hard to explain certain things to American doctors. Frenzel directed women with children to go to the left, and then walked over to the men with a whip in his hand. "Tailors step forward!" he shouted. Tojwełe was short, thin, fourteen years old, and he was not a tailor. He didn't have a chance during the selection. He looked at Frenzel's back. He said, "I want to live." He repeated this several times. He spoke in a whisper, but Frenzel turned around. "*Komm raus, du kleine*," he called out in Tojwełe's direction, and ordered him to join the men who were staying there. Blatt testified about this at the trial in the Hague.

Frenzel was at liberty during his trial. During a break he asked Blatt if he could talk with him. They met in a hotel room.

"Do you remember me?" Blatt asked.

"No," Frenzel said. "You were so young then."

Blatt asked why Frenzel wanted to talk with him.

"To apologize to you," said Frenzel. It turned out that he wanted to apologize for the 250,000 Jews who were gassed in Sobibor.

5

Blatt was a witness for the prosecution in a couple of other cases. Among them was the case of the Gestapo chief in

Izbica, Kurt Engels. The one who had placed the crown of thorns on Blatt's father's head. Tojwełe used to clean his motorcycle for him. It was a magnificent machine, with a sidecar and two gleaming fenders on either side. Each fender had a skull carved into it. Engels insisted that the skulls be polished to a shine. Tojwełe cleaned them for hours on end. It was an excellent job because when he was cleaning the motorcycle no German would bother him, even during a round-up. Engels had one other Jewish boy, Mojszełe, working for him. He was from Vienna. He took care of the garden. Engels would talk with him about caring for the flowers. He was fond of him. You're a fine boy, he used to say. You'll be the last to die and I'll personally shoot you so that you won't suffer. Blatt testified during the investigation that the Gestapo officer had kept his word. After the war, Kurt Engels opened a café in Hamburg. It was called Café Engels. It was the favorite gathering place of the local Jews. The Jewish community of Hamburg used to hold their celebrations in one of its rooms. He was unmasked in the 1960s. Blatt gave sworn testimony during the investigation. At the end, he was shown fifteen men and the prosecutor asked which one was the accused. Engels smiled. He still has a gold tooth, said Blatt. When he placed that crown of thorns on my father, he laughed with that gold tooth.

After the confrontation, Blatt went to take a look at the Café Engels. He introduced himself to the owner's wife.

Did he personally kill anyone? she asked. Did he murder children?

The next day, the prosecutor questioned both of them, Engels and Blatt. A clerk came in; Mrs. Engels was requesting a moment to talk with her husband. She walked over to her husband, took off her wedding ring, handed it to him without a word, and left the room.

The next morning the prosecutor phoned him. Kurt Engels had poisoned himself in his cell and Blatt wouldn't have to come to a hearing.

6

All night they walked through the woods. In the morning, Peczerski took their weapons and the nine strongest people. He said they would go and scout the area and he ordered the others to wait. He left them one rifle; Staszek Szmajzner had it. He had studied to be a jeweler in the ghetto, brought his tools along to Sobibor, and made signet rings with beautiful monograms for the SS. He got hold of the rifle during the uprising. He was an excellent shot; he killed several of the guards. Peczerski asked him to stay with the people in the woods.

Peczerski did not come back. Blatt saw him forty years later, in Rostov on the Don. Why did you leave us? he asked. As an officer, I had a duty to go to the front and continue the fight, Peczerski replied. He had found a group of Soviet partisans. He fought till the war ended. After the war, he was sent to prison. People from Sobibor sent him invitations, but he could not get a passport and never traveled abroad. He was living with his wife in a communal apartment, in a multifamily house. They occupied one room. A large tapestry, which he himself had embroidered, hung above the bed. It depicted a dog. A sheet was hanging in a corner, behind it a wash basin and toiletry articles. Our rebellion was an historic event, and you are one of the heroes of that war, said Blatt. Did they award you any decorations? Aleksander Peczerski opened the door to the hallway, looked around, shut the door, and whispered, Jews aren't given decorations. Why did you take a look outside? asked Blatt. After all, your neighbor is a friendly woman. It's always best to check, Peczerski whispered.

7

When it became apparent that Peczerski would not return, they split up into small groups. Each one set out in a different direction. Tojweŀe, together with Fredek Kostman and Szmul Wajcen, set off through the woods in the direction of Izbica. The next evening they noticed a village. A light was burning in one of the windows, in the fourth house on the right. A family was seated at the kitchen table—a tall, very thin man with pale hair; a short, heavy-set woman; a girl Tojwełe's age; and a somewhat older boy. A holy image hung above them. In it, too, people were seated at a table, but they were all men. They wore white robes, and each one had a golden halo. The halo was largest over the one who sat in the center, his index finger raised. My father, Leon Blatt, was a Legionnaire, said Tojwełe. All those people in the painting were Jews, said Szmul. Every last one of them. We have something for you to remember us by, said Fredek, and placed on the table a handful of jewels that he had taken from the sorting room in Sobibor.

The farmer, Marcin B., made a hiding place for them in the barn. In the evening he would bring them a pot of food. They could hear his slow, heavy steps in the distance. He would stand still in the middle of the barn, check to see if any strangers were there, and approach the hiding place. He'd remove the straw and bend back the nail; only he knew which nail could be bent. He would take out a board; only he knew which board was not nailed down. He'd place the large, cast iron pot on the threshold. One of the boys would stick out his hand and drag the pot inside. The farmer would put the board back in place, bend the nail back, and straighten the straw. They sat in darkness. Fredek and Szmul talked in a whisper, and Tojwełe listened. Tojwełe was small, red-haired, and freckled. True, before the war he used to smear himself with Halina brand anti-freckle cream that he'd stolen from his mother, but without results. The other boys were two years older than he was; they came from big cities and they didn't have freckles. They talked eagerly about the cars that they would buy after the war. Fredek was going to buy a Panhard, and Szmul, a Buick. This was the first time Tojwełe had ever heard those names. He interjected that he would buy an Opel, the same kind that Captain Lind owned. An Opel! The boys burst out laughing disparagingly and began reminiscing about railroad stations. Some of them were approached through long, dark tunnels, and thundering trains passed overhead. Did you ever see a tunnel? Tojwełe had to confess that there wasn't a single tunnel in Izbica. Half a year passed. Marcin B. told them it was spring already and the apple tree was in bloom. It grew near the barn, next to their hiding place. There will be a lot of apples, Marcin B. said. He asked where they had gotten such nice sweaters and a leather jacket. From Sobibor, from the sorting room. They lent him the jacket and a sweater. He went off to church on Sunday, wearing them. On Monday, several men came to see him. They screamed, Where are you hiding the Jews? We want leather jackets, too. They probed the straw in the barn with sticks, but they didn't find anything. Maybe their sticks were too short. You heard them, Marcin B. said that evening. Go away from here; I'm afraid. They asked him to buy them a gun, and then they'd go into the forest. They'll catch you, he said, they'll ask where you got the gun and you'll betray me. We won't betray you; please buy one. You'll definitely betray me; go away, I'm afraid.

A couple of days passed. In the evening they heard the farmer sending his children to their grandparents' for the night and calling the dog into the kitchen. Later, he came to the barn. He bent back the nail, removed the board. Fredek crept out to get the pot. They saw a bright light and heard a crash. Fredek curled up and his legs began thrashing. Someone's hands shoved Fredek to the side. They saw the chubby face of a boy they didn't know and another light. Tojwełe felt a sting in his jaw. He touched his cheek; it was wet. He, too, was shoved aside by someone's hands. When he opened his eyes, in addition to the darkness he saw Uncle Jankiel. He was sitting beside him on the straw, tiny and hunchbacked as always. Aha, Tojwełe thought, I am seeing Uncle Jankiel. When someone's dying, he sees his own childhood, so I'm dying now. You know, said Uncle Jankiel, a person's hair and fingernails keep growing for three days after he dies. He can hear, but he cannot speak. I know, said Tojwełe, you already told me. I am no longer alive; I can still hear and my fingernails are growing. He heard voices and crashing sounds, one after the other. Make sure he's dead, or he'll start moaning when morning comes. That was the farmer's wife talking; who knows, maybe she was talking about him, about Tojwełe. Mister, please let me live; I'll be your servant for the rest of my life. That was Szmul talking. The men didn't want Szmul to be their servant, because there was another bang and Szmul fell silent. He's already getting stiff. That was Marcin B. talking, undoubtedly about

Tojwełe, because he touched his hand. Here it is! That was an unknown voice, maybe belonging to the boy with the round face. He must have found something. Probably their bag of gold, because suddenly they all jumped up and ran to the kitchen. Are you alive? That was Szmul. No, Tojwełe whispered. He wanted to tell him about the hair and fingernails, but Szmul had begun crawling to the door. He got up on his knees and crawled after him. Szmul turned toward the trees. Tojwełe had the impression that he was still following him, but when he came to, he was sitting under a tree, at the edge of the woods. He got up and walked straight ahead.

8

The Wieprz River flows through that district.

The river divided the world into two parts: the good and the bad. The bad part of the world was on the right side and that's where Przylesie was located. On the left side of the river were the good villages: Janów, Mchy, and Ostrzyca.

In the good villages, many people were saved—Staszek Szmajzner, the tailor Dawid Berend, the saddler Stefan Akerman, the meat sellers Chana and Szmul, the grain dealer Gdali from Piaski, the windmill owner Bajła Szarf, and the children of Rab, the miller, Estera and Idełe.

The miller's children were saved by Stefan Marcyniuk.

Twenty years before, he had escaped from a Bolshevik prison in the heart of Russia; in Poland, he settled down in the attic of a Jewish-owned mill. "If I had a sack of flour," he said, "I would bake bread, sell it, and I'd have a couple of groschen." The miller gave him a sack of flour, and Marcyniuk baked bread. He earned his couple of groschen, and in later years he was one of the richest farmers in the entire region.

The miller and his wife died in the ghetto; their daughter, Estera, was sent to Sobibor. On the day before her planned escape, Estera's mother appeared to her in a dream. She came into the barracks and stood over her bunk.

"Tomorrow, we're running away from here," Estera whispered. "Do you know about this?" Her mother nodded her head. "I'm afraid," Estera complained. "I don't know where to go; they'll surely kill everyone."

"Come with me," her mother said, and taking her daughter by the hand, she led her to the exit. They left the barracks and passed the camp gate. No one shot at them.

"After all, this is only a dream," Estera thought. "Tomorrow they'll shoot and they'll kill everyone." They walked across the fields and through the woods and stopped in front of a large farmyard.

"Do you recognize it?" her mother asked. Estera recognized it; they were in front of Stefan Marcyniuk's house. "Remember this," said her mother. "This is where you must come."

They escaped on the following day. Eleven days later

Estera and her fiancé reached the village of Janów and stood in front of the house from her dream. It was night-time. They didn't want to awaken the owners, so they crept into the barn and lay down on the straw.

"Who are you?"

They heard a man's voice in the darkness and someone's hand grasped Estera's hand.

"It's I, your sister," Estera said, because that was the voice of Idełe, her older brother.

"It wasn't your mother, it was God who sent you," Stefan Marcyniuk said, when they told him the dream. "You'll stay with me until the war is over."

Tojwełe, too, reached good people in a good village, on the left bank of the Wieprz. He found a place to stay in Mchy with Franciszek Petla. Petla's uncle was President Mościcki's valet. He had traveled with the president to Romania, came home, and opened a porcelain booth at the Różycki bazaar. The village was informed that Tojwełe-Tomek was the valet Zięba's own son. This impressed the children in the pasture, especially Kasia Turoń, who was the tallest girl, because she took after her father the cavalry soldier. The children looked after the cows. Their favorite game was "Catch the Jew." The "Jew" was chosen by counting out one-potato, two-potato; the "Jew" ran away, and everyone chased him. When he was caught, he'd be asked: "Are you Jude? Did you kill Christ? Bing bang!"

Two Germans stopped Tomek in the meadow. He was walking with Stefan Akerman, the saddler, who was in hiding in Ostrzyca. One of the Germans blocked them with his bicycle. "Jude?" The boys who guarded the cows and Kasia Turoń were sitting nearby.

"Mr. German," Kasia shrieked, "that's our lad."

"And this one?"

Kasia didn't know Akerman.

"Mr. German, don't you know what to do? Drop his pants and bing bang."

Akerman dropped his pants. The German removed his rifle and held it out to the children. "Who wants to make bing bang?"

The children were silent.

"Do you want to make bing bang?"

The German held out his rifle to Kasia. She shook her head. The other German took Akerman away into the woods. They heard a shot. That German came back, then both of them got on their bicycles and rode away. At night, Akerman came to see Tomek. The German had given him a cigarette, fired into the air, and told him to walk away.

In the morning, in the meadow, Kasia said, "It's my fault, isn't it?"

She was pretty. Maybe not as pretty as Małka Lerner, but she had blue eyes to make up for it.

"Tomek, will you come to our drying shed? As soon as it gets dark. You'll read to me."

He expressed surprise. "I can't read in the dark."

"You can, you can," said Kasia.

He couldn't read, so they lay down on a pile of tobacco. It smelled lovely. Kasia still felt bad because of Akerman, so Tomek consoled her. Then he felt bad, and Kasia consoled him. Then she screamed, "Tomek, you're a Jew!"

He jumped up and fastened his trousers.

"Don't worry, I won't tell anyone," she whispered hastily.

She told her brother Andrzej. He started giving Tomek Polish lessons.

"We don't say 'Ojej, what's haaa-pening?'; we don't draw out our vowels, and no 'ojej.'"

Andrzej Turoń belonged to the Armia Ludowa, the communist People's Army. After the war he joined the militia. Two AL partisans in Mchy joined the militia—Turoń and Tadzio Petla, the farmer's nephew. They came home for the first postwar Christmas, both of them in uniform, and someone fired a burst of bullets at each of them. Tadzio was seventeen and Andrzej eighteen. No one knew who shot them, and if someone did know, he's no longer alive, says Romek, Franciszek Petla's son. (The youth with the round face, whom Marcin B. took on as his helper, also signed up for the militia and someone fired a round at him.)

Romek Petla is a leather worker. He lives in the Nowe

Miasto district in Warsaw. He sits at an old Singer sewing machine and sews the uppers for knee-high boots. Blatt visited him this time, too. They each drained a shot glass and followed it with a bite of something. They reminisced about Mchy, Romek's deceased father of blessed memory, the Jews, Kasia, and also that postwar girl from Tarzymiechy, a little one, but with what eyes, and also, naturally, the bullet in the jaw.

"Are you keeping it there?" Romek Petla asked.

"Yes, I'm keeping it," said Blatt.

"And do you remember how I brought you bandages and salve? I got them from the German. For two eggs."

Romek Petla placed boot tops with sewn-in linings onto a level pile. The linings were insulated. The boot tops were ugly. For cheap boots, for poor people. Romek Petla said the demand for them keeps growing because there are more and more poor people. But so what, since the boot tops exude boredom. Romek Petla poured out another glass for each of them, but it was of no help for his boredom. On the contrary. For some reason, boredom takes root most eagerly in parts of shoes—in the soles, linings, and uppers.

"So why do you really hold onto that bullet?" asked Romek Petla.

"Do you think I know?" Blatt sank into thought. "I lose everything. If I had it removed, I would lose it, and this way it sits in my jaw and I know that it's there."

9

The war ended. The surviving Jews from Izbica got together in Lublin. For some ill-defined reasons it never occurred to them that they could return to Izbica. It also never occurred to Tomek, but he couldn't leave. His boots remained in Marcin B.'s barn. He was walking around barefoot. The war was over, but he was barefoot. He gave ten zlotys to a boy.

"Go to Przylesie," he told him, "go into the fourth house on the right and ask for Marcin B. Tell him that Tomek is waiting for his boots near the well in Maliniec. Say that Tomek's boots remained in the barn."

He waited near the well. It was July. It was hot. Marcin B. arrived, also barefoot. He held in his hands tall boots, polished to a shine. They were Szmul's boots. Without a word he held them out to Tomek, turned around, and walked away. Tomek took the boots and also walked away. Still barefoot. With Szmul Wajcen's boots in his hands, the right boot in his right hand and the left in his left hand.

He went to Lublin. He met Staszek Szmajzner, the one to whom Peczerski had given the single rifle in the woods.

"You have splendid boots," Staszek observed.

He told him about Fredek, Szmul, and Marcin B.

Staszek stopped a Soviet truck carrying a captain. He gave him a half liter of vodka. They drove to Przylesie. Marcin wasn't there. He's gone to do the threshing, his wife said. You can stand in for him. Staszek indicated

Marcin B.'s daughter with his head. Gentlemen, the wife groaned. She ran off somewhere and came back with gold in a pot. Take it, gentlemen. The girl was already standing against the wall. She isn't guilty, Tomek yelled. And my sisters, were they guilty? asked Staszek. Was my mother guilty? Marcin B.'s wife sank down on her knees before Staszek. He raised the rifle he'd taken from a German to his eyes and took aim at the girl. Tomek shoved his arm. Marcin B.'s wife was weeping loudly. Marcin B.'s daughter stood there calmly, leaning against the wall. She was looking up at the sky, as if she wanted to discern the flight of the bullet.

10

They lived on Kowalska Street, with Hersz Blank, who had established his own business in Lublin. Come what may, people will always need hides. Someone stopped Tomek in the stairway: "Don't go there; there's still blood." He wasn't surprised. He knew that people exist, exist, and then they're gone. He went to the Jewish cemetery. Hersz Blank lay in the little cemetery hut, wrapped in linen. A boy from Sobibor, Szlomo Podchlebnik, had brought him there and wrapped his body. Jews from Izbica, Lublin, and Sobibor came for the funeral. At the funeral people talked about two things. That this was done by men from the Armia Krajowa, the Home Army, and that it would be necessary to leave here. Many people left for Palestine. Tomek went to the States via Palestine, because he knew an American Jew. He settled in California. At first he worked on automobile radios. Then he began speaking about Sobibor, he wrote a book about Sobibor, and placed memorial tablets in Sobibor. Twenty-odd years later, his wife informed him that she didn't intend to spend the rest of her life in Sobibor.

Staszek Szmajzner left for Rio. He married a Miss Brazil. He settled down in Copacabana. When he opened his windows, he could hear the Atlantic. He left his home and moved to the Amazon. He didn't want to see any people other than Indians. With his rifle that he acquired in Sobibor and with which, in Marcin B.'s homestead, he had fired an honorary shot for his mother, his sisters, and also for Fredek and Szmul, he shot at birds in the Amazon jungle. He spent thirty years writing a book. When he finished it . . . and so forth.

The Home Army men who were involved in the Hersz Blank affair were executed in April 1945. Not because of Blank, but for a conspiracy against Bolesław Bierut and the authorities. Bierut personally approved the sentence. It was carried out in the Lublin castle. Eleven people were executed during a fifty-five-minute period. They were young people, patriotic and brave. The Supreme Court recently absolved them of all the crimes they were accused of. Several articles appeared in the press in relation to this. All of them included references to Blank. The journalists agreed that since it was Home Army people who killed him, they must have had a reason. Evidently, Blank was an agent of the UB, the secret police. One journalist wrote: "One may assume that Blank was suspected of being an informer." Another journalist didn't assume. He knew that the Home Army men suspected Blank of collaboration. The third journalist was certain: Hersz Blank was a collaborator with the UB.

In the meantime, the Home Army men were charged not with Blank's murder but only with participation in his murder. The murderers were not sentenced at all. Even their names were not mentioned during the investigation. Pseudonyms were used: "Rabe" and "Mietek." Why weren't their names revealed? Why weren't they charged? Why did the authorities guard these secrets till the end?

Who killed Hersz Blank is not known. Home Army soldiers? Members of the UB? Or perhaps murderers hired by the security organs, either the Polish or Soviet ones?

No one is trying to explain this death. The Supreme Court, which declared the innocence of the Home Army men, dismissed the Blank case as beyond the statute of limitations.

Hersz Blank was twenty years old. He was religious, from a Hasidic family. When he was murdered, his older brother was sitting over the Talmud, as was his custom, talking with God about the most important matters.

11

Thomas Blatt parked the car before entering the village.

We walked through a ravine.

Along the right side, there were houses at intervals of about two hundred meters. If you have to ask for food, these are the kinds of houses to approach, Thomas Blatt said with expertise.

A forest stretched along the left side. If you want to disappear, this is the kind of forest you need.

He believed that he would recognize the trees from behind which they saw the light in Marcin B.'s house. And also the trees behind which Szmul Wajcen had disappeared. That was obviously absurd. Those trees had long since been chopped down for fuel.

He began counting how many shots had been fired. First one, at Fredek. Then another, at him. Then many shots, but how many? Four? Three? Let's say four, so six altogether, two plus four. But what if there were five shots? Then it would have been seven all told. At the same time, he was counting the houses. When we passed the third house, he became noticeably agitated. "Oho," he kept repeating, "the fourth house will be soon."

With every passing year there were fewer traces. At one time, the walls were still standing; then only the corner room (by some strange chance, it was "their" corner room, with the hiding place), then the foundation, then only rubble—rafters, boards, stones.

This year, there was nothing. Nothing. Other than an unpruned apple tree with crooked, rheumatic limbs. Thomas Blatt wasn't even sure if he'd found the right place. He walked back and forth, looked around; the brush and grass reached his chest. There was no such brush growing anywhere else in the area.

We walked straight ahead. We noticed a farm. An old woman was standing in the yard. I said that I was collecting material for a book. About what? Oh, about life. This wasn't a precise answer, but she invited us into her kitchen. It turned out she was the sister of Zosia B., Marcin B.'s wife. Blatt was again preoccupied with arithmetic. If she heard shots, how many were there? She knew immediately what he was talking about. She hadn't heard, but Krysia Kochówna, who was spending the night with them, had said, "There was shooting at Uncle Marcin's last night." At night, the sound of a shot carries well, very far, and you can hear it. "In the morning people in every house knew that the Yids had been picked off. Three of them were lying there, but do you know what? One had risen from his grave and walked off. No one knows where he is."

"He's here with you." Blatt couldn't contain himself, although I had begged him, before we went in, to sit quietly. "With you, in your kitchen." They looked at him with disbelief. "Check it out, if you like. Here's the bullet, right here."

They came over to him, one after the other: Zosia B., the sister, the sister's daughter, the daughter-in-law. My, oh my, a bullet. Can you feel it? Because I do. It's really a bullet. Comforted, they rushed to make sandwiches. So, you're alive. Help yourselves. And did you give them a lot of that gold? My, oh my. Because our Józik found a ring with a heart in their farmyard, a big one that fit his middle finger. He lost it in the army. But I told him, Don't take it, Józik. And my daughter lost the bracelet that a Jewess from Maliniec left her as a memento. She came with her child, we gave her milk, but we couldn't take them, because we were afraid. The little girl was big; she could talk. And what did she say? She said, Mama, don't cry. Here, help yourselves. Two Jewesses were hiding in Dobre, in the woods. People brought them yarn and they knitted it; then someone denounced them, and they hanged them- selves right there. A beautiful Jewess lay in the road be- yond the bend. First she was dressed; then someone took her dress. People came to look at how beautiful she was. Marcin, too, disappeared together with his wife and chil- dren. On the day when the uniformed men came from Lublin. The horses were neighing, the cows were mooing, the grain was standing there, but everyone was afraid to go in and everything was going wild. Perhaps he's no longer alive? Or maybe he bought a farm with that gold? Or set up a mushroom-growing cellar? And why are you look- ing for him? Could you kill him now? I couldn't, said Blatt. Do you want to ask him about something? I don't. Then why are you looking for him? To look at him. That's all, just to look. To look? And is that worth it to you?

12

A Jewess with a child. A beautiful Jewess. Two Jewesses in Dobre. Fredek in the barn. Szmul in the woods. . . . Thomas Blatt began counting again. They are all here, he pointed all around, and there are no graves. Why are there no Jewish graves? Why is no one sad?

We passed Izbica, Krasnystaw, and Łopiennik. The sun was setting. Everything was even uglier and older. Maybe because specters are wandering about. They don't want to leave, since no one mourns for them, since no one weeps for them. From unlamented specters there is such a grayness.

Only a Joke

1

When he was twenty years old, he started to write a book. It was a book about his childhood. His childhood had lasted seven years, until the Warsaw Uprising. He is still writing this book. For thirty-five years he has been writing a book about a childhood that lasted seven years.

2

The world that he decided to write down took place in a spacious apartment, in a large Warsaw apartment house.

There were three rooms: a golden room, with walls the color of honey, with toys on an étagère, and a teddy bear with shoes (his father took one of those shoes for good luck when he went to join the uprising); a dining room, filled, as he described it, with mature bronze, in which the furniture was enormous and full of inner strength, while the fragile delicateness of glass was sheltered behind the panes of a credenza; an office, with a gloomy library, with paperweights in the shape of ships, and with the surging waves of seas in a couple of paintings.

Within this stage set existed the world that was to become his theme.

3

After a year or two, the thought occurred to him that his book was complete. He retyped it, reread the typescript, and when he put down the last page he understood that everything had to be a lot better. It should be like Tolstoy's *Childhood*. Or like Proust. He was in his fourth year of law school. Since his studies might interfere with his continuing work on the book, he abandoned his studies and began correcting the book. Alas. By now, all the rooms were peopled with spirits; his beautiful mother, sunk in thought, paced back and forth in the dining room, eternally waiting for his father who never returned; his kindhearted aunt told fairy tales, always with a bad ending; in the golden room, grandmother dozed in her armchair, and her faithful maid was always about to set the table—he extracted these spirits by force, by their hair, from the nooks of his memory, from cracks, and it still was not Proust, despite everything.

He was working in a store at that time; at night, he worked as a guard transporting goods. Since work interfered with his writing even more than his studies had done, he returned to the university and completed his master's degree—with distinction, in fact.

He became a legal adviser in an important institution. Realizing that marriage would assure him the peace that is essential for writing, he married a classmate. He bought a dog, a coarse-haired terrier. He drilled holes in concrete walls and hammered in pegs to support storage shelves. This task did not disrupt his concentration; on the contrary, it helped. He began to go for long Sunday walks with his wife and dog.

4

First he gave up on the storage space. He'd already measured and cut the paneling, but he had to record the day on which his aunt told the fairy tale about the death of the nightingale. It was the first time he'd heard the word "death" and he immediately decided to find a profession in which he would never die. Pilot was ruled out, sailor was ruled out, even trolleycar driver didn't seem safe, so he asked his father in what profession you never die, and his father . . .

Next, he gave up the Sunday walks.

Next, they were late for Easter breakfast with his wife's parents. He was already standing in the anteroom, dressed in his holiday clothes, ready to go out, when he recalled how very dissatisfied he was with grandmother's presence in the rocking chair, in the golden room. She will reprimand him any moment now for the noise, he thought. No games work out when grown-ups are present, but it turned out that not only did grandmother not punish him, she wasn't looking in his direction at all. He played louder and louder, the old lady still kept silent, until finally he knelt beside the chair and stealthily peered into her face. His wife was already taking the keys out of her pocketbook when he, looking closely at the old woman in the rocking chair, understood that he had not seen such a face on any grown-up. He saw the abandoned house from which they all had left; he saw the empty rooms, one after the other, growing ever smaller, disappearing into the distance like a long chain into the depths of time.

"Are you coming?" his wife asked, but he was thinking with regret that the woman in the rocking chair was long since gone, that she would never respond to him who was kneeling beside her.

They arrived at his inlaws' toward the end of Easter breakfast. His mother-in-law was crying; his father-in-law said nothing. When they got home he said, "From now on you will go there by yourself," and he returned to the woman with the empty face in the rocking chair. When he suddenly heard her quiet voice, "Thread the needle for me," he felt an enormous sense of relief, took off his holiday suit, and brewed himself some fresh, strong tea.

Next, he moved out of the house. He rented a room in which he found quiet and concentration. When his money ran out, he went home and asked his wife if she could move back home with her parents for a while. She moved, but she had to come back, because martial law had just been declared and people had to live where they were registered.

5

One day his wife's girlfriend asked if a man from Solidarity could spend the night at their place. He was in hiding; a warrant had been issued for his arrest. They found a newsletter from the conspiracy with a photo of the man, took a good look, and told the friend that he could come to them.

The man from the underground arrived in the evening. They talked with him until late at night and even gave him some chapters from the book about childhood to read. The man from the underground was surprised that the word "I" was repeated in it so often; they went to sleep; in the morning they told their guest that he could stay longer.

The man from the underground lived with them for several months, moved out for a while because of the danger, then came back to live with them again. Every day his comrades or other people who were being pursued came to see him. This must have been going on for a couple of years, because the man was already there when they had the old dog, who was paralyzed and blind, and whom he found slightly disgusting, and he was there later on with the new, black and yellow dog, whom he would sometimes lift into his lap. They asked him what was really the sense of hiding like this. He answered that he didn't know himself, maybe not much sense, sooner or later they would be found and would go to prison, but they couldn't behave differently because they would be betraying the people who trusted them.

He didn't like the thought that the man from the underground would go to prison. That meant that they, too, would go to prison, and he didn't like thinking about prison at all. They don't give you paper. Is it possible that he would have to give up writing his book for a couple of years because of the man from the underground?

He worked in a frenzy. Behind the wall, in the little room, the man with an arrest warrant out for him was discussing something with his colleagues; his wife was moving about in the kitchen, trying not to make any noise; he was sitting in the main room and writing his memories of childhood.

He loved the world to which he was transported by his writing. It was safe; everything was in order; he was in order in that world; no one expected anything of him— that he would study, that he would earn a living, panel the storage space, go to his inlaws', and hide a man from the underground. In the spacious rooms of that world he hammered nothing, he hid no one, and despite all that, he was in order.

In the past, he had strived to unearth every detail in his memory. He had tracked them like a hunter stalking birds in the forest; if a bird fell, he picked it up, looked it over and delighted in every little feather. Now he gave up on new birds and kept on describing, over and over again, the same walls, the same furnishings, the same events. His mother was waiting for his father. His aunt was saying, "The nightingale died." He was asking, "Died? What does that mean?" His grandmother was asking him, "Thread the needle for me." A man handed over a pistol. Mother was waiting for father. The nightingale died. "Would you like to shoot?" the man asked.

SHOOT?

At first, he didn't recognize the man and didn't understand his words, but slowly a forgotten scene that he had not yet described even once emerged from memory.

The uprising was in full swing.

They were all sitting in the cellar.

The golden child's room resembled a large barricade.

A tall man, dressed in civilian clothes, with a red-and-white armband, handed him the pistol. "Would you like to shoot? Then shoot. . . ."

There were Germans in the next building. They had an excellent sharpshooter whom it was impossible to kill. For days on end there were conversations about how to lure him out and who would finally kill him. When the man said, "Would you like to shoot?" he immediately imagined that he, a seven-year-old boy, would kill the expert German marksman with his first shot.

"Here," said the tall man. "Hold it. Here's where you squeeze. Yes, right there."

With the pistol that barely fit into his hand, he slipped over to the window. Through a slit between the drapes and the wall, he spotted the balcony of the neighboring building. On the balcony stood a man. He was bending down; it looked as if he was watering flowers. The man was wearing a German uniform. He thought that he was imagining everything; after all, you couldn't see that much through a slit.

"Well?" The tall man was impatient. "Are you going to shoot?"

Again he raised the pistol; the man in the German uniform was standing with his back to him, bent over the flowers.

"But I could kill him," he whispered, terrified.

"Then kill him," the man laughed.

He got up from behind his desk and went into the kitchen.

"Listen," he said. "Now I know how my book should end. I've remembered a very important scene. There'll be nothing after this scene. Do you understand? Childhood will end, the book will end . . ."

"Wonderful," his wife rejoiced. "Sit down and write."

"How can I write?" He was furious. "They could come for him tomorrow." (This was during a short absence of the man from the underground, who was supposed to return the next day.) "They'll take him away. They'll take us away. Can you picture it? I'll be in prison, without tea, without paper, and that scene, which I cannot write, with which my book is supposed to end."

"Are you moving out again?"

"No," he replied. "HE won't come here any more. Go to them. Say that . . . Whatever, but go at once. And I'll take a leave without pay, I'll sit down and finish my book."

6

He took a leave without pay and began to describe the golden room, transformed into a barricade for the uprising.

It turned out to be harder than he'd thought, because he didn't remember the most important details.

Where was the huge brown credenza that had been moved out of the dining room?

How had the fragments of a crystal glass that was kept in the credenza scattered?

Where was the bear from the top shelf? (He was lying there without shoes, so what had happened to the other shoe?)

And the sea paintings that were removed from the office? In what place had the expert German marksman drilled holes in the surging waves?

He remembered nothing. Long, extended labor awaited him.

The man from the underground never returned to them.

7

One day, during his evening stroll, he heard the howling of a dog and a girl's scream. He set off in that direction. He saw two young men. One was beating the dog; the other was twisting the girl's hands behind her back.

He shouted, "Leave them alone! Well? Will you leave them alone?!"

Both men turned away from the girl and the dog and ran toward him.

He remembers that they were holding a stick.

He remembers that he was lying on the grass.

He remembers that, protecting his face with his hands, he thought, "Fortunately, they're wearing running shoes."

He remembers the voice, "You might kill him."

And the other voice, "So I'll kill him."

8

He came home from the hospital.

He hasn't taken up his memories yet.

He is under the impression that he has already tracked down all the birds, but, although they are lying dead all around him, he doesn't feel like bending down for them.

9

His favorite author is Conrad, and his favorite book *Lord Jim*, but it doesn't occur to him that refusing the man his house, that abandoning the man from the underground, ought to remind him of Jim's escape from the deck of the "Patna." He also doesn't think that there was any connection between the affair of the man from the underground and his struggle to defend the girl and her dog.

10

He believes that he will be judged some day for two things: how he lived and how he acquitted himself in the mission that was assigned to him. Everyone has a mission, only one doesn't always or immediately understand it. Sometimes the task is unclear and one has to expend a great deal of effort in order to deduce its meaning.

Kafka's *The Trial* is not a metaphor for totalitarianism, as Havel suggests; that would be too simple. It is the trial that awaits each of us, and life is an accumulation of defense material for the coming judgment.

So, he will be judged on how he lived: how he offended his wife, shoved a dog off his lap, and denied his home to a man from the underground.

And he will be judged on his mission, his writing.

Under one condition, naturally.

That God not guffaw at the sight of him and cry out, "Writing? But that's a joke! It was only a joke that you treated seriously. Well, well, don't be angry. I did it out of pity. So you could live. You don't think, do you, that you would have known how to live your life without writing?"

The Back of the Eye

1

The village is situated in a bowl. A local artist produced picture postcards depicting an unchanging, unblemished panorama. The dark green of forested hillsides, the brighter expanse of a meadow, the red of sloping rooftops above white houses, and across the center a strip of bright blue, the Murg River. The river rises in the nearby mountains and flows into the Rhine. The mountains are part of the Schwarzwald massif.

On one of the postcards the artist photographed a bench. Constructed of four boards and painted red, it stands to the side, beneath a tree.

The boards were probably from the local sawmill. They look old. It is not impossible that they were cut from trunks that were taken to the sawmill by French soldiers.

They brought them there after the war. No sooner had they occupied the village than they started trucking timber down from the forest. (What did the French liberators need those boards for? Tables? Coffins? A bridge? A dance floor?)

Stanisław W., called Stani by both the French and the Germans, arrived in the village shortly after he was liberated from the concentration camp. He worked in the sawmill. It may well be that it was he who sawed the boards from which the red-painted bench was constructed.

2

The French soldiers and their captain lived in a small house in the center of the village. They took their meals in the former café. Gizela worked upstairs from the café. She worked for a family. She had excellent qualifications. The convent school of the Franciscan Sisters provided a comprehensive education for future maids: sewing, cooking, infant care, cake-baking (the local specialty was the famous Black Forest chocolate cake, a unique composition of sponge cake, cherries, cherry liqueur, chocolate, and cream), and impeccable manners. How to sit down on the edge of a chair in the presence of a count; how, listening to the countess's orders, to bow one's head . . . The graduates had no trouble finding positions in the best families, and, as the world war came to an end, the best families fled ahead of the advancing front, taking their servant girls with them.

Gizela worked for a family that had escaped from Düsseldorf. The family lived on the second floor; the former café, occupied by the French, was on the ground floor, and Stani frequented that café.

Stani was tall and diffident, and he danced the foxtrot better than anyone in the entire village. The first time Stani and Gizela went to a dance, it turned out that the best dancer among the women was a refugee from Prussia. It is quite likely that the refugee from Prussia was in love with Stani, but she had three children and was waiting for her husband who had not yet returned from the eastern front. Most certainly, it was not a matter of any importance.

Stani and Gizela moved into one of the white houses with a red, sloping roof. It can be seen on a postcard. On the same postcard one can see the spire of the church that Stani used to go to with his Polish prayer book, the flat roof of the laundry where Gizela worked, and also a tourist hotel. The tourists were not rich. Wealthy people traveled to nearby Switzerland; the village's guests were the exhausted inhabitants of the Ruhr Valley. Dressed in shorts and hand-knit woolen knee socks, they strolled conscientiously through the neighboring forests and inhaled deeply.

They loved these forests—praise be to God. Thanks to them, Gizela had work all year round.

Stani didn't want to go back to Poland. His mother was no longer alive and he was under the impression that he would not like the communists. He also didn't want to remain in Germany. They planned on going to Australia, but every time they were packed up and ready to leave they had to unpack their suitcases in a hurry, because Gizela was pregnant again. They stayed in the village—praise be to God. What would she have done in a foreign country with four children and without Stani?

3

Stani was neat, hard-working, and didn't like to talk. He didn't talk about the war or about Poland, but sometimes he asked questions.

"Did you know that there were concentration camps?" he asked Gizela.

"No, I didn't know," she answered.

"What about your father?"

She answered, "Mama didn't allow him to discuss such things."

Shortly before the end of the war she had seen people in striped clothing in Düsseldorf. They were getting out of a truck; they were terrifyingly skinny, and passersby threw them packs of cigarettes that they concealed under their clothing with trembling hands. Two men in black uniforms came running over, with whips and shouts. The passersby scurried away. She was shocked. She hadn't imagined that a man could be so skinny.

She described that scene for Stani: "I thought they were from a normal prison. How could I have known they were from a concentration camp?"

"It's good," Stani replied, "it's good that you didn't know."

She asked him, "What exactly ought I to know?"

"Nothing."

"What do you mean, nothing? If you think I ought to know something, why don't you tell me?"

She didn't understand it. Stefan, their son, didn't either. When Stefan grew up, he asked her, as Stani once had asked, "Did you know there were concentration camps? And what about your father?"

Stani told her about two incidents—how they'd had to run around the barracks, barefoot, in the snow, in the frost; and how they used to count off during a roll call: One—two—THREE—four—five—SIX—seven—eight—NINE. The prisoners who were numbers three, six, and nine stepped out of the ranks and the count began again: One—two—THREE—four—five—SIX. When it was over, the threes, sixes, and nines left the camp and the rest of the prisoners went off to work.

People said that the threes, sixes, and nines were working in a village, for a *Bauer*. Stani envied them. He dreamt about the lighter work and country food and prayed that the count of three, six, or nine would fall on him at the next roll call. His prayer was not heeded. After the war he learned that the threes, sixes, and nines had not gone to a *Bauer*; they'd been shot.

She told Stefan about this when he grew up, but her son was angry at Stani: "He could have fought. Why didn't they defend themselves?"

One day Stefan said, "Mama, I think I finally understand him."

This was many years after Stani's death. She was talking with Stefan through a thick, bullet-proof glass panel. The glass divided the cell in two; it was set into large, steel frames on top, bottom, and sides. There were slots in the two side frames. Sound passed through them muffled and dull, and in addition the glass in the pane sometimes behaved like a mirror. At those moments, instead of seeing the person on the other side, one saw one's own reflection. It was to this pane of glass, to himself reflected in the glass, that Stefan said in a muffled, unintelligible voice, "Mama, I think I finally understand him."

"What do you understand?" she shouted at the glass.

"Him. I've been reading . . ."

"What?" she repeated several times, but she could not make out his answer.

The guard signaled that the visit was over.

4

Before the war, Stanisław W., his siblings, and parents had
lived in Łódź. His father was a weaver. They'd rented a
room in a garret; it was narrow, long, with a tiny window
and a sloping mansard wall. In it were beds for seven
people, and when the grandparents were still alive, for
nine. In addition to the beds there was an iron stove with
a stovepipe, a basin for washing and two buckets, one for
clean water and the other for waste. On the floor under
one bed, potatoes were stored. On the floor under another bed, they stored coal. There must have been some
chairs, at least one, because during the war, when his
mother came home from smuggling, all frozen and wet,
his father would seat her on that chair, wrap her in a blanket, and place a tin basin with burning alcohol by her feet.
The children would gather round and look at the flicker-
ing blue flame, while their mother thawed out.

Stanisław W.'s younger brother remembered the apartment. After the war he moved to a small town in the western territories. He worked in a uranium mine. It was shut
down a couple of years later. While it still existed the town
was a secret military zone; outsiders were not permitted
to enter, and soldiers checked the documents of passengers arriving on intercity buses. The brother's wife worked
in a carpet factory. The carpets are still nice-looking, but
production is declining and they're beginning to lay off

workers. They have too many kilims, all of them depicting the Madonna of Częstochowa, 1 meter 20 cm by 90 cm. They are sold to the workers for 170,000 zł. each; on the free market the price can be as high as 1,000,000 zł. They tried weaving the Madonna of Ostrobrama, too, but the gold color came out too dull; there were problems with the dye. Recently, something has gone wrong with the legs of Stanisław W.'s younger brother. Many people in the town have something wrong with their legs: without warning, they collapse onto the floor and are unable to stand. Some people say it's because of the uranium ore slag piles; others say it's from the Chernobyl fallout, which was heaviest in nearby Śnieżka; and still others say it's from vodka.

The younger brother was a child during the war and doesn't know why Stanisław wound up in a camp.

First, their father was taken away to forced labor. Then their mother took the children to the country and concealed her oldest son in a haystack, but he was found and sent to forced labor. In the autumn of 1940 their aunt, their mother's sister, came to see them and brought some food. By then their father and Stanisław W. were gone.

The following autumn their aunt was standing at the window and whispering the names of the dead for whom a mass would have to be ordered on All Souls' Day: Father, mother, sister Czesława . . . She shuddered: Why Czesława? She's alive, after all. At that very moment she caught sight of her sister through the window, walking toward them down the middle of the street. She was pretty and young, just as in the past. "What am I seeing?" their aunt marveled, and hastily threw the window wide open. She leaned out. "Czesiu!" she called, but there was no one in the street. A few days after All Saints' Day she received a letter: "Dear Auntie, please come, Mama is dead and the street is feeding us."

The younger brother knows where their mother is buried: the fourth section, fifth row, nineteenth grave. That's what the gravedigger told the children, so they could memorize it. They repeated in a chorus: "Fourth section, fifth row . . ."

Stanisław W.'s mother was thirty-five when she died. She was on her way home from smuggling; she had stopped off in Łódź at a friend's home and asked for some tea. The friend went into the kitchen and when she returned with a glass of tea, their mother was lying on the floor.

The mother looked older than thirty-five. The photograph shows a thin woman, hunched over, with a haggard face and tired eyes. The woman was trying to smile at the camera lens, but what came out was a grimace that emphasized the wrinkles around her mouth and her sunken cheeks.

She had a modest funeral on a chilly, cloudy day. In the photograph one can see a small group of people near the excavated grave, earth, a painted coffin, and the gravedigger's rope sling.

Beside the grave stand small, sad children.

Behind the children stands a tall youth, staring at the coffin.

That youth is Stanisław W.

He was taken away for forced labor while his mother was alive, but he was standing over the coffin.

He had said something to Gizela about running away from forced labor.

Perhaps he escaped to get to the funeral, and they punished him by sending him to the concentration camp. Only how did he know that his mother had died?

Perhaps he saw her as a young, pretty woman, as she had once been, walking down the center of the street? But he could not have remembered his mother as young and beautiful. Rather, he saw that thin, hunched-over woman, with a grimace at the corners of her mouth.

Stanisław W.'s sister-in-law asked if he and Gizela had met during the war. If so, he might have wound up in the concentration camp because of Gizela. When the sister-in-law was in forced labor, they hanged a lad in the square for having had a romance with a German girl. They drove all the Poles into the square; they had to stand there until the end and hear how the lad pushed away the noose and screamed at the hangman. The sister-in-law doesn't know how to spell this in German, but it sounded like *"Lass mich leben, lass mich leben . . ."* So, if Stanisław W. and Gizela met during the war . . . But no, they met after the war, at a dance. When it turned out that Stani danced the foxtrot better than anyone in the village, so well that he didn't need to dance with that refugee from Prussia at all. They must have sent him to the camp for something else.

5

He was in three camps; it's not known when and for how long. In the archives in Warsaw there's a card file from Dachau: small pink and yellow slips of cardboard, made by Polish prisoners after they were freed from the camp. Drawing upon their own sources of information and memory, they inscribed on each card a prisoner's name, his camp number, where he came from, and where he was sent to. There are eighty-five cards with the surname W. in the archive—the most popular Polish surname after Kowalski. There are seven cards with the name Stanisław W.

Stanisław W. from Bolimowo came from the Flossenburg camp; he was handed over to the Gestapo. Stanisław W. from Pieścirogi came from a camp in Działdowo and was sent on to Mauthausen. Stanisław W. from Sierpc, Stanisław W. from Zielonka, Stanisław W. from Anielino, Stanisław W. from Horbaczów, Stanisław W. from Kutno. He arrived in a group transport and was sent on to the camp in Natzweiler.

Stanisław W. from Kutno was Gizela's future husband and Stefan W.'s future father. The camp number checks out: 122962.

Stanisław W. died on October 9, 1953, at 7:30 a.m. in a clinic in Tübingen. Thanks to the autopsy records we know that he was 180 cm tall, weighed 79.7 kg, and suffered from chronic glomerular nephritis.

He was twenty-seven years old.

6

Gizela spent the last week in the clinic. On the last day the professor entered, looked at Stani, and gave orders to transfer him to a private room. Stani comforted her: "Tomorrow, I'll be better, you'll see." He started to doze off, then woke up: "Tomorrow, I'll be better."

When she came to, she understood that she was already at home, sitting at the table and holding her arms around a small cardboard box. In the box was Stani's clothing and a tattered Polish prayer book: *We Sing to the Lord.*

7

Dark green, bright green, a stripe of blue, the tall roof of the hotel. Gizela washed dishes and cleaned rooms; the flat roof of the laundry—Gizela folded and packed men's shirts . . .

The tourists' favorite occupation was going for walks in the neighboring forests. The children's favorite occupation was throwing pine cones at the tourists. The director of the school summoned Gizela: "Your son is throwing pine cones at our tourists."

"All the children throw them," said Gizela. "Why are you complaining only about my child?"

"Your daughter," the director of the school said on another day.

"Your son . . ."

"Your daughter . . ."

"It's because the other fathers," Stefan explained, "were war heroes."

Gizela was upset. The other children told stories about their hero-fathers—beautiful, noble stories. The fathers fired guns, primarily on the Eastern front. The fathers perished, but to the last drop of their blood . . . And what could her children tell them? That their father dreamed of being a number THREE or SIX? Could a father who ran barefoot around the barracks and prayed that one of those numbers . . . Could such a father be compared with heroes of the Eastern front? Could the son of such a father arouse kindly feelings in the director of the school?

(A woman from their village whose birthday is the same as Stefan's sends him a greeting card every year. As a postscript she adds one sentence, always the same: "If it weren't for the director of the school, you would have grown up to be a decent man." Stefan already has twenty-odd cards from that woman and twenty-odd times that sentence as a postscript: "If it weren't for the director of the school . . .")

"Anyway," the other mothers told the other children, "if his father was in a camp, there was a reason for it. Hitler or no Hitler, nobody was sentenced without a reason."

After yet another incident when Stefan ran away from school, Gizela requested advice from pedagogues. These were pedagogues in the Department of Youth Services. They advised her to entrust her son to a reformatory. "He'll wind up there sooner or later," the pedagogues said, "but if you hand him over voluntarily, it will be easier to get him out when he wises up."

Stefan says he was in the reformatory for a year.

Stefan sits in an isolation cell, in a particularly well-guarded part of the prison known as the Maximum Security Section.

He's been in this cell for twelve years.

After twelve years of isolation, the past has become blurred in his mind; space and time are foreshortened. It is sixty kilometers to the city where Gizela lives now; it seems to him that the city is nearby. It seems to him that he was in the reformatory for one year, but the documents in his case file—the case for which he's serving time in the Maximum Security Section—clearly show that he spent six years in the reformatory.

8

The director of the reformatory was a pastor, a tall man with a puffy face and strong fists.

The pastor gave his charges three grades every week: for work, for studying, and for behavior. The lowest grade was six and the highest, one. If someone got even one six, he spent the weekend in an isolation room. There were two boards in it. You could sit on the lower board; on the upper board, you could rest your arms and head.

From time to time the boys in the reformatory would try to escape, but they soon returned, brought back by the police. After their return they would talk about what was happening on the outside. One of the youths, who had run away to Frankfurt, told them that university students were protesting against the corrective methods employed in reformatories. A girl had written a film script about this, and some people wanted to establish a juvenile home with entirely different methods.

The screenplay girl was named Ulrike Meinhof, and the girl with the entirely different methods was named Gudrun Ensslin.

9

After Stani's death Gizela petitioned the authorities: Her husband had died as a result of kidney disease; the illness was the result of his stay in a concentration camp. Stani W.'s four children, Gizela wrote, deserved compensation.

Gizela W.'s attorney was informed that he should apply to the Office for Compensation Requests in Baden-Württemberg.

The Office requested the records of Stanisław W.'s illness from the clinic.

The clinic was unable to confirm that Stanisław W.'s illness was a consequence of his time in the camp. In particular, the back of Stanisław W.'s eye yielded no conclusive evidence. The clinic requested an opinion from the Institute of Pathology.

The Institute of Pathology was unable to confirm anything.

The attorney appealed the negative decision.

Gizela W. wrote a letter: "Does the German state believe that my children should drop dead? I am not a beggar; I am fighting for what is owed me."

The attorney regretted that Mrs. Gizela W. had written such an inappropriate letter.

The Office for Compensation Requests rejected the request because the deceased did not meet the conditions of §1.2, but suggested that she could petition for compensation under §167.

Eight years after Stanisław W.'s death the mayor of Cologne informed Mrs. Gizela W. that: The government of the Federal Republic of Germany had signed an agreement with the High Commissioner of the United Nations to the effect that persecutions based on ethnicity would be subject to new legal regulations.

The mayor of Cologne informed Mrs. Gizela W.: "There is no proof that the deceased was persecuted for political reasons, for reasons of race, belief, or ideology. If he was persecuted, it was for reasons of ethnicity. This compensation is not transferrable to the heirs."

10

During her first prison visits Gizela used to say to the bullet-proof glass with the openings on both sides: "If your father were alive, he would certainly not praise you for this. When the Americans liberated the camp they put a stick in your father's hands and said, 'Take revenge.' And do you know what your father told them? 'Thank you, gentlemen, but I am not suited for such things.'"

After his visits with his mother Stefan got into the habit of carrying on lengthy conversations with his father.

"They gave you a stick, not a machine pistol," Stefan would begin. "It was only a stick. Why didn't you want to take it from them?"

He wasn't sure of his father's answer. "I am not suited . . ." is not a sufficient answer, so he would start over: "No doubt you thought that the world had to change after Dachau. All right then, take a look at this world. Look at the fists of the director of the reformatory. Look at the two boards in the isolation cell. Look at me, sitting on one board and resting my head on the other. And remember, too, my mother's face whenever she came back from the bureaucrats in charge of compensation. OK, so you didn't want a stick, but I beg you, take a good look at my mother's face."

He addressed his father with growing indignation. As if there existed a connection between the director's fists and the stick his father didn't take, the bureaucrats dealing with compensation requests and the isolation cell in the Maximum Security Section.

11

From the life history included in the case records: He worked on a ship for a few months. For two weeks he was a machinist. He established contact with left-wing radicals. He took part in a demonstration against the Minister of Justice. He contributed his unemployment compensation to a fund for the defense of prisoners. He was connected with persons who were preparing a terrorist attack on the German Embassy in Stockholm. He joined the underground of the RAF—the Röte Armee Faktion or Red Army Faction.

From the case files: Members of the RAF rented several apartments in the area. They stole a yellow Mercedes and bought a white minibus. They prepared two Heckler & Koch carbines, one Polish-made WZ 63 machine pistol that took Makarov cartridges, one Colt revolver . . .

At 5:30 p.m. a blue Mercedes carrying Dr. Hanns Martin Schleyer and his driver drove up, followed by a white Mercedes with three policemen. They turned right, and then a yellow Mercedes drove off the sidewalk and into the roadway. Dr. Schleyer's driver braked. Men leaped out of the minibus and opened fire on the driver and policemen; they dragged out Dr. Schleyer, who was not wounded, and drove off in a westerly direction. The attack lasted two minutes. The driver and the three policemen died on the spot. The driver took five bullets, one of which was fatal; the first policeman was shot twenty-three times, two shots causing fatal wounds; the second policeman was shot twenty-four times, three of them fatal; the third, twenty times, three of them fatal—in all, a total of one hundred bullets. All the fatal shots were administered with 9-mm Makarov cartridges. This happened in Cologne, on September 5, 1977.

Hanns Martin Schleyer was the president of the Employers' Association of the Federal Republic of Germany. In exchange for his freedom, the hostage-takers demanded the release from prison of ten RAF terrorists, among them Andreas Baader and Gudrun Ensslin.

On October 13 four Arab terrorists hijacked a Lufthansa airplane; they landed in Mogadishu and repeated the demands of the RAF.

On October 17 German commandos freed the passengers and killed three of the hijackers. The pilot died, shot by the terrorists.

Several hours later, prison guards in Stammheim found the corpses of RAF members Baader and Raspe, who were dead from bullet wounds. Gudrun Ensslin was hanging in a window. It was determined that she had committed suicide.

Two days later, Dr. Schleyer's corpse was found in the trunk of an abandoned Audi 100.

Seven months later, in 1978, Stefan W. was arrested at Orly Airport and charged with the abduction and murder of Hanns Martin Schleyer.

The trial took place in 1980. Stefan W. refused to testify about the abduction and murder, but he gladly expressed his opinions about the actual aims of the German bourgeoisie, the tentacles of neocolonialism in the Third World, and the Vietnam War, which revealed the true face of American imperialism. He was sentenced to life in prison without parole.

12

The terrorists were surrounded with hatred and fear. It was feared that they were producing an atom bomb and would want to use it. Polls showed a rapid rise in proponents of the death penalty. Gudrun Ensslin's ten-year-old son was splashed with muriatic acid. It happened during his school vacation. The boy was playing; it was adults who threw the bottle. His face was burned. He was taken to the United States. American doctors performed three skin transplants. They were successful; the doctors were experienced because they had operated on soldiers who were burned by napalm in the Vietnam War. Not one cemetery would bury the trio of terrorists from Stammheim. People demanded that the bodies be cremated and the ashes scattered, or else that the remains be thrown into a landfill. In the end, they were buried in a cemetery in Stuttgart, at the mayor's request. The mayor was Manfred Rommel, the son of Field Marshal Rommel, the Desert Fox from the North African campaign and participant in a plot against Hitler. The mayor appealed to mercy. Because he was a Christian. Because among the dead was Gudrun, his neighbors' daughter. Because long ago, in Ulm, Gudrun Ensslin's parents lived two houses away from Manfred Rommel's parents.

Mr. Ensslin was a pastor. After the war his daughters, Christiana and Gudrun, had asked the same question that Stani asked Gizela W.: "DID YOU KNOW?"

Unlike Gizela, the pastor knew. He knew the Stauffenberg conspirators; they belonged to his parish. He knew the circumstances of Rommel's death in the nearby stone quarries.

His daughters were angry at him for not having denounced the crimes. He should have denounced them publicly, from the pulpit, during services.

The pastor explained that the Gestapo were present at services.

"That's no reason to have kept silent," his daughters replied.

13

Christiana Ensslin, her hair clipped short, with sunken black eyes and wearing a stretched-out sweater, lives with a terrorist who served sixteen years in prison and then was pardoned by the president. She is friends with a woman terrorist who is still in prison, but is already partially pardoned: she spends the nights in prison, while during the day she sews costumes for *La Traviata* at the city opera. When she receives her complete pardon she will go on vacation to visit a Swedish princess known as the Angel of Prisoners. Christiana Ensslin is an activist in the Union of Film Workers. She fights for greater funding for women directors. She would love to finance a film about Rosa Luxemburg's first day of freedom. It is 1918; Rosa leaves the Breslau prison, boards a train, travels to Berlin, enters the editorial office, greets Liebknecht, sits down at her desk, and starts writing. She is writing an article about the situation in Germany. That's all very well, but who will go to see such a film? "I will," says the terrorist who was in prison for sixteen years. "I will," says the terrorist who sews costumes for *La Traviata*. "I will," says Christiana, whose father did not condemn the crimes. "I will," says Dr. Ronge, who translates for our Polish-German conversations. "I will," I say, although I have no intention of going to see a film about Rosa Luxemburg's first day of freedom. I say this out of sympathy for skinny, neurotic Christiana Ensslin. And that would have been the entire audience.

14

The Maximum Security Section was built especially for Stefan W. and his friends from the RAF. It is located in the depths of the prison, in Ossendorf, in the northern part of Cologne. No daylight enters the cells. The walls are made of sound- and odor-absorbing materials. Keys don't jangle, the combination locks don't creak, and the coffee that Stefan W. brews has no aroma. Stefan has brought a thermos with boiling water and little jars to the visitation cell. He shakes out some Nescafe and sugar from the jars, stirs them for a long time, gradually pours in boiling water from the thermos, and makes cappuccino. The visitation cell is a concrete container, decorated with several pictures. They portray Peter the Great on his stone horse, a review of the troops on Senate Square, and a bridge on the Moika in winter garb. The pictures were put up by Stefan's warden, a fellow by the name of Hemmers, who nurses a fondness for Petersburg.

Stefan was mild-mannered; he had gray-green eyes and a trusting smile like his father. He greeted me with *"Dzień dobry, pani"* and then switched to German, having exhausted his fund of Polish words. He said that he was in Poland only once, at the airport, changing planes. When he and his friend entered the transit lounge, they noticed a most wanted list on the wall with a photo gallery of terrorists whom the police were searching for. They had no trouble finding their own photographs. Luckily, no one paid any attention either to the photos or to them; they were told to board their plane half an hour later. His second contact with Poland was via the intermediary of that Polish WZ 63 machine pistol. It was purchased abroad. It was a very nice gun, because it was small, not that much larger than a revolver. His colleagues loved it because it was easy to conceal.

Unfortunately, it has a serious drawback: its cartridges are too short. He wouldn't have a chance in an exchange of bullets with a NATO pistol. Makarov cartridges can be used only in a Polish gun. The policemen and Schleyer's driver were shot with Makarov cartridges. Stefan W. said that the driver was definitely not supposed to die. That was a mistake. The policemen also were not supposed to die, but no one knew that there would be policemen. Previously, Schleyer had not had a police detail; they had begun guarding him shortly before the kidnapping after another attack, on a bank director. In short, a botched job. Although, on the other hand, said Stefan W., when a person takes a gun into his hands he has to accept the fact that he will kill.

There were more than a dozen victims of the actions that began with the abduction of Schleyer: his driver, the three policemen, the three airplane hijackers, the plane's captain, the Stammheim prisoners . . . Yes, Stefan W. agreed, many victims. But it had never occurred to any of them that the government would not accede to their demands. It simply never entered anyone's mind. They had long since known that imperialism is bloodthirsty, but they didn't think it was that bloodthirsty.

15

For the first time in sixteen years, Stefan W. left the Maximum Security Section and came to the general prison visiting hall. It was a fairly large room with two doors. One door opened to allow the prisoners to enter; their guests were ushered in through the other door. Each prisoner was accompanied by a guard. The guard held a card that he placed on a table. At the table, facing the hall, sat a woman supervisor. She was a corpulent brunette wearing gold earrings and a low-cut top edged with black lace. She wore a skirt that buttoned down the front. The bottom buttons were undone so that the skirt revealed her thighs, which were so heavy that the supervisor couldn't bring her knees together. She sat there with her legs, encased in black patterned tights, spread apart.

In addition to the supervisor's desk there were six tables and chairs in the hall. The prisoners were led in first. They were predominantly young men. They entered slowly, looking around, holding plastic bags with their dirty things in their hands. The visitors were admitted afterward. They were women. They entered more quickly, running actually, pushing chairs out of the way and throwing themselves into the men's embraces. They wore long, loose skirts. They sat with their backs to the hall and immediately began talking. They would listen for a moment to the men's responses, burst out laughing, and continue telling them about whatever it was.

Stefan W. began by explaining the sources of RAF ideology. It is derived from guerrilla movements, from urban partisan struggle in South America. Nowadays, imperialism feeds on exploitation of the Third World. The people of the RAF are those in Western Europe, in the very center of imperialism, who act in support of the Third World and its liberation movements.

"We attack the bastions of imperialism," said Stefan W. "Military bases, banks . . ."

The women were moving from the chairs onto the men's knees; now their long skirts flowed to the ground and shielded them like screens. Their laughter changed into fitful, muffled giggling.

"Mao taught that the working class in imperialist countries is no longer a revolutionary class," Stefan W. continued. "And it profits from the exploitation of the Third World. The revolutionary subject of society . . ."

The women were unfastening the men's buttons; the giggling slowly subsided.

". . . became the people of the social margins. The homeless, the unemployed, former prisoners, youth from reformatories. We have to rely on them in our struggle."

The women began rocking on the men's knees, gently, like boats on calm water; in the visiting hall of the prison in Ossendorf only Stefan W.'s voice could be heard:

"The marginalized must organize!

"We demand the factories!

"When the capitalist summons the police we will respond with force!

"Marx said that violence is the midwife of a new world. Freedom is only a question of time!"

The woman supervisor began making signs. The visit

was over. The women slowly fastened their own and their men's buttons, arranged their blouses and their hair.

"Eastern Europe?" Stefan W. now spoke more softly, lost in thought. "Why does Europe matter? One failed experiment. The idea is alive. Millions of people in the whole world still suffer from poverty. The idea is alive . . ."

The guards came to collect the prisoners. The hall emptied out.

16

His conversations with his father, conducted in his maximum security cell, ended in a silence behind which Stefan W. could feel a stubborn, unreconciled disapproval. At first this had rankled. In time he realized that it made no sense to keep on arguing with him. One cannot persuade a person who survived Dachau without fighting back and who then sought justice in a slim book with the title *We Sing to the Lord*. He turned to another person. To Czesława, his father's mother, his grandmother. She had worked like a dog. She was poor. She was exploited by factory owners. She was a person whom Stefan W. and his friends wanted to defend against the exploitation of capitalism. She had to be an ally in his struggle. She had to understand him. He could feel her sympathy and turned to her with unlimited trust. He missed her. He didn't know how old she was. He could not know that, dying, she was younger than he was, sitting here on his prison bunk. Had he known the story told by Stanisław W.'s younger brother about the room in the garret and the basin with the burning alcohol, he would certainly have addressed the woman seated in the chair. The frozen woman, wrapped in a blanket, with a blue flame at her feet like an eternal flame.

17

One day, Stefan W. received a letter from an unknown correspondent. She wrote that she was twenty-three years old, was fighting for women's rights, sympathized with him and would like to visit him. He invited her to come. She was tall, slender, dressed in a black sweater and black leather pants. They conversed through the bullet-proof glass about women's rights, world imperialism, and love. Since then she had visited him once a month and wrote him letters and postcards several times a week. There was never a beginning or an ending in these letters. She would begin in midsentence, even in the middle of a word, and end in midsentence. They could guess each other's mood from the handwriting. They had an agreement that they would not pretend. When she was sad she did not attempt to smile, and when she looked ugly she did not put on makeup. They were afraid that they thought better of each other than they should; that they were creating idealized images of each other. That was their constant worry and an unvarying theme in their conversations.

"You probably think that I am good," she would shout to the glass. "Please, don't think that. I am a lot worse than you would like me to be."

"You probably think that I am wise," she shouted another day. "I am getting stupider all the time."

"You probably think . . ."

For seven years they could not touch each other. They made love with their eyes through the bullet-proof glass.

For three years they met in the visitation cell, in the Maximum Security Section, under the depictions of Petersburg in the winter.

One day, she wrote that she was in love with another man. Since they had sworn not to pretend to each other, she would not deceive him and would never write again.

She kept her word.

He calculated that she had come to see him over ten years, so she must be thirty-three already.

He couldn't count the letters and cards she had written over five hundred weeks.

18

Daniel Cohn-Bendit, the leader of the Paris students in 1968, was recently named director of the Intercultural Department attached to the Frankfurt mayor's office. He has a spacious office with a secretary who brings in coffee and flaky pastry. He said that terrorism derives from the atmosphere of the fifties and the silence at that time about the war. Young Germans wanted to know what it had been like, but their parents had said, "Why open old wounds?"

Only in 1963, at the trial in Frankfurt of the Auschwitz war criminals, did people begin to speak publicly about those crimes. When the war in Vietnam began, Andreas Baader, Gudrun Ensslin, and their colleagues said, "We will not be silent like our parents." They started to commit murders. They believed they had the right, in revenge for Vietnam, to murder American soldiers who were stationed in West Germany, and to murder a German judge in revenge for bourgeois justice. They believed they were on the side of right. When someone is on the side of right, everything he does is just and even murder becomes a sacred act. Andreas Baader summoned Cohn-Bendit, the hero of 1968, to join in a common struggle. Cohn-Bendit told Gudrun Ensslin and Baader that it is a crime to entice youth from the reformatories into the RAF. He denounced terrorism. In the first place, he didn't like murder. In the second place, he didn't like Andreas Baader and had no intention of building a new, better world with him.

The government dealt with the terrorists in a cruel fashion. The SPD, the Social Democratic Party, was in power, and it had promised Germans that the year 1933 and the weakness of the social democrats would never be repeated.

The terrorists said, "You will never accuse us of silence."

The Social Democrats said, "You will never accuse us of weakness."

"It was a psychodrama," said Cohn-Bendit. "A German psychodrama, in which both sides were reacting to Nazism."

19

One of the cards sent by the girl in the black sweater was a reproduction of a painting by the Mexican artist Frida Kahlo. Stefan W. liked it; he wrote to the company that had printed the postcard. The publisher sent him a new reproduction and a letter: "You have a Polish surname. Are you interested in Polish affairs?" In the next parcel there were German translations of a couple of Polish authors.

From then on Stefan W. started reading Polish books about the Second World War. He became interested in the Warsaw Ghetto. He decided that there was a similarity between the Jews in the Ghetto and the prisoners in the concentration camps. He read a book about the ghetto by Władysław Bartoszewski, and Kazimierz Moczarski's account of his conversations with Jürgen Stroop, and also Czesław Miłosz's poetry. He and the girl thought about why there were disparities between Jürgen Stroop's version of the uprising and Marek Edelman's in *To Outwit God.*[1] Or, why Edelman doesn't like communists even though they were the first to send a gun to the ghetto, the one with which the Jewish police commander was shot at. He gave all the books to the girl to read; she hasn't returned some of them to this day, perhaps out of forgetfulness, perhaps for other reasons. Marek Edelman became the greatest authority for him. It distressed him that a leader of the uprising in the ghetto thinks of the terrorists' contempt for human life as a posthumous victory of Nazism.

He said, "It's a shame that I didn't know about this before."

20

The best day for Gizela W. is Sunday. She doesn't work, she doesn't assist her elderly neighbor lady, and she doesn't meet with the parents of other RAF prisoners. (She doesn't like these meetings. Only professors and doctors attend; she is the sole worker among them.)

1. *To Outwit God*, Hanna Krall's interview with Marek Edelman, was originally published in Polish as *Zdążyć przed Panem Bogiem* (1977). The English translation, by Joanna Stasinska Weschler and Lawrence Weschler, first appeared under the title *Shielding the Flame: An Intimate Conversation with Doctor Marek Edelman, the Last Surviving Leader of the Warsaw Ghetto Uprising* (Henry Holt, 1986) and was reissued as *To Outwit God* (Evanston, IL: Northwestern University Press, 1992). [*Translator's note*]

First she eats her Sunday breakfast. Then she writes a letter. That her legs are less painful. That she still has enough strength to help the old lady. That the chestnuts by the river are in bloom, and any day now the Japanese cherry blossoms will come out. She seals the envelope and writes the address: Ossendorf, the prison.

Next, she prays. She starts with thanks: that it's a new day, that her legs are less painful, that the chestnuts by the river . . . , after which she presents her plea. Not to God; she wouldn't dare to burden Him with her concerns. She addresses her plea to Stani, who endured so much, never complained, and went to church every Sunday. He is undoubtedly dearer to God than she is, and if Stani should ask Him God will not refuse and will allow her to remain alive until her son returns.

She addresses herself to Him directly, and not through Stani, about only one of her concerns.

When she asks that He forgive their son his terrible sin.

Proofs of Existence

The Dybbuk

1

Adam S., tall, handsome, blue-eyed, with a white-toothed smile, teaches the history of architectural design at an American technical college. He's spent time in Poland. He had an interest in the wooden synagogues that burned down during the last war.

I asked Adam S. why an ambitious, six-foot-tall American, born after the war, would be interested in something that no longer exists. He answered in a letter. It was composed on a computer. It seems he was in a rush, because he didn't tear off the perforated edges on either side. His father, he wrote, was a Polish Jew who had lost his wife and son in the ghetto. After the war he moved to France and married again. His new wife was French. Adam was born in Paris, and they spoke French at home.

"So, what draws me to Poland?" he wrote in that computer printout. "A dybbuk. My half-brother, my father's son from his first marriage, born before the war and bearing my name, who somehow was lost in the ghetto. He has been inside me for a long time, throughout my childhood, my school years. . . ."

The word "dybbuk" is borrowed from Hebrew; it signifies a connection. In Jewish tradition it is the soul of a dead person inhabiting a living human being.

Adam S. realized quite early that he was not alone. He would be visited by outbursts of inexplicable fury, another person's fury; at other times sudden laughter, not his own, would overcome him. He learned to recognize these moods, acquired fairly good control over them, and did not betray himself in the presence of other people.

From time to time this subtenant would say something. Adam S. didn't know what he was saying, because the dybbuk spoke in Polish. Adam S. began studying the language; he wanted to understand what his younger brother was telling him. When he had learned enough, he came to Poland. That was when he developed an interest in the architecture of the wooden synagogues that had existed only in Poland, for three hundred years. Heavenly gardens, marvelous beasts, the walls of Jerusalem or the river of

Babylon were painted on their walls. Their domes, invisible from the outside because they were concealed beneath ordinary roofs, created a feeling inside of infinite, vanishing space.

Those gardens and walls had long since disappeared; Adam S. viewed them in old, damaged photographs, but he wrote beautiful essays about them. Eventually, he earned a doctoral degree and got a position at a better college. He married. Bought a house. Lived like any normal, educated American. Except for that double life of his—his own life, and that of his younger brother, who had been named Abram, and who, when he was six years old, "somehow was lost in the ghetto."

2

In April 1993 Adam S. came to Poland. He hadn't been here in several years, so first he visited Połaniec, Pińczów, Zabłudów, Grójec, and Nowe Miasto. Who knows why. Maybe he hoped that this time he would see the river of Babylon in the synagogue in Grójec, and the willow trees upon which "we hanged our harps . . . in the midst thereof." Maybe in Zabłudów he hoped to rediscover the gryphons, bears, peacocks, winged dragons, unicorns, and water snakes.

As was predictable, he found grass and a few pathetic trees.

He returned to Warsaw. The ceremonies marking the fiftieth anniversary of the uprising in the ghetto were just getting started. We went out for dinner during a break between scholarly panels.

I congratulated Adam S. on the birth of his first-born son, looked at his photographs, and asked, "What about . . . him?"

I didn't know what word to use—brother? Abram? the dybbuk?

"Is he still there?"

Adam S. understood immediately.

"He is. He sticks with me, although I'd be happier if he left. He butts in, kicks up a fuss, doesn't know himself what he wants. He's unhappy living with me and I feel worse and worse with him.

"I found out," Adam S. continued, "that there's a Buddhist monk living in Boston. An American Jew who converted to Buddhism and became a monk. My friend told me, 'This man might be able to help you.'

"I went to the monk. He had me lie down on a couch and massaged my shoulders. At first I didn't feel anything, I just lay there, but after half an hour I suddenly burst out crying. I had never cried like that in my adult life. I listened to that cry and I knew that it wasn't my voice. It was the voice of a child. It was the child crying in me. The crying grew stronger and I started screaming. The child started screaming. He was screaming. I could see that he was afraid of something, because it was a scream of terror.

He was terrified, he was in a rage, he thrashed about, waving my fists. Obviously, he was exhausted; he'd quiet down for a few minutes, but then he'd begin again. This was a child who was out of his mind from exhaustion and terror. Samuel, the monk, tried to speak to him, but he wouldn't stop screaming. This went on for several hours. I thought I would die; I didn't have any strength left. Suddenly I felt that something was happening inside me. Something was rocking in my innards. The scream subsided and a shadow flickered over my abdomen. I knew that all this was only in my imagination, yet the monk must have noticed it, too, because he addressed him directly.

"'Leave here,' he said calmly. 'Go to the light.'

"I don't know what that was supposed to mean, because all this was taking place in ordinary light, during the day.

"'Go . . .'

"And the shadow began moving off. Samuel didn't stop speaking; it was just a couple of words, always the same: 'Go to the light . . . Go on . . . Don't be afraid, you'll feel better there. . . .'

"And he went. He didn't so much walk, as slip away, further and further, and I understood that in another minute he would be gone completely. I felt sad.

"'Do you want to leave me?' I asked. 'Stay with me. You are my brother; don't go away.'

"It was as if he'd been waiting for this. He turned back and with one swift movement he leaped inside me, and I couldn't see him any more."

Adam S. fell silent.

We were sitting in an Asian restaurant on Theater Square. Outside our window, the day was chilly. All the days of the anniversary ceremonies were permeated with damp and chill. A drizzly grayness had settled on cars; people were rushing somewhere, not bothering to look around. We watched them, thinking the same thought: Does anyone care about ghetto ceremonies, wooden synagogues, and crying dybbuks?

"No one cares about them in America, either," I concluded, although Adam S. knew this better than I did.

Snapshots of Adam S.'s wife and son lay on our table—a happy, bright-eyed boy in the arms of a serious woman, her brown eyes visible through thick lenses.

"Moshe," said Adam S. "Like my father. But my father was an actual ordinary Moshe, and we call the little one Michael."

"Did you tell your father about the monk and Boston?"

"Yes, in a phone conversation. He was living in Iowa; I called him after I got back home. I thought he wouldn't believe me, that at the very least he'd be taken aback, but he wasn't taken aback at all. He listened calmly, and then he said, 'I know what that cry is. When they threw him out of the hiding place he stood in the street and cried loudly. That was the cry—the cry of my child who was thrown out into the street.'

"This was the first time I had talked with my father about my brother. Father had a weak heart; I didn't want to upset him. I knew that my brother had died, like everyone else; what more was there to ask about? Now I found out that the boy had been hidden somewhere with his mother, my father's first wife, along with a dozen or so other Jews. I don't know where, if it was in the ghetto or on the Aryan side. Sometimes I picture a kitchen and people crowded together. They were sitting on the floor, trying not to breathe. He started crying. They tried to quiet him. How do you calm a crying child? With candy? A toy? They didn't have toys or candy. His crying grew louder and louder, and the people crowded together on the floor were thinking the same thought. Someone whispered: 'We're all going to die because of one little kid.' Or maybe it wasn't a kitchen. Maybe it was a cellar, or a bunker. My father wasn't with them; only she was, Abram's mother. She stayed with the others. She survived. She settled in Israel, maybe she's still living there, I didn't ask, I don't know. . . .

"My father died.

"My wife went to the hospital to give birth. I went with her and lay down on the bed next to hers. When the midwife told my wife, 'Push, any minute now,' I felt something happening inside me. I felt movement, a rocking motion. I guessed who it was. He was getting ready to leave me. He was getting ready to take up residence in my child. I leaped up from the bed. 'Oh, no,' I said out loud. 'Don't you dare. No ghetto. No Holocaust. You are not going to inhabit my child.'

"No, I didn't shout, but I did speak forcefully. I spoke in Polish, so the midwife and my wife didn't understand. But he understood. He grew calm, and I lay down again. I was so exhausted that I fell asleep. I was awakened by a loud cry, but there was no terror in it. It was the cry of a healthy, normal baby who had just come into the world. My son. Moshe."

3

The Buddhist monk sat on the bed, his legs extended stiffly. Both legs were encased in white plaster pipes; only his toes, long and restless, protruded from them. He was holding a flute that was a yard long. From time to time he raised it to his lips; his toes, protruding from those pipes, would begin to flutter and bend in time to the music, and the room would be filled with high, mournful sounds.

The monk had two flutes, both of them made of cedar. The shorter one, of white cedar, was a gift from some North Dakota Indians; the longer one, of red cedar, came from Arizona, from the mountains. The two woods can be distinguished by their fragrance.

"Check it out." He moved the flute over to me. It was saturated with a dizzying aroma, full of mysteries that aroused no fear.

In the monk's room there was a bed, a wheelchair, two crutches, a hotplate, a mug on a little table, and a few books. I thought: I have already been in such a room, in a medieval castle, in Germany. In the home of Axel von dem Busche, a baron and an officer in the Wehrmacht. He saw how the Jews were being killed in Poland and he resolved to kill Hitler. I recognized the smell of the bedding, the coffee and medicine.

I said, "I have already been in such a room, but it was a German baron without a leg who was sitting on the bed."

The monk grew animated. He, too, had befriended a German, but not a baron. A communist, who had fled Hitler and come to the States. The man taught Buddhist philosophy in Washington. He protested against the war in Vietnam, and in 1968 he supported the young people who were demonstrating against it. He was expelled from the United States for his radical views. For his fascination with Buddhism, Samuel Kerner, a Jewish boy from the Bronx, is indebted to Edward Conze, a German communist.

It was the sixties. Sam and his college friends had shoulder-length hair and wore sandals on their bare feet; they looked with loathing upon American wealth, especially in their own homes, took LSD, and waited for the revolution. The revolution was supposed to be worldwide, in defense of justice and against the rich. Later they were called the New Age generation, or the Age of Aquarius, which would arrive with the new millennium.

As well-read people they already knew that revolutionary purity does not last long. Politics creeps in after the initial rapture, and the revolution devours its young.

They had three options:

Go to a poor country, in South America, for example, and organize people for the struggle.

Hold up American banks and distribute the money to the poor.

Slip away with the goal of perfecting mind and character in peace and quiet.

They chose to perfect themselves.

When the revolution goes bad, when the rapacious struggle for money and power begins, they will emerge from their seclusion pure, ennobled, resistant to temptations, and will rescue the ideal.

They had no idea where to go in search of perfection, so Samuel asked Edward Conze for advice.

"You are a Jew," said Conze. "Reach for your own tradition."

So Sam went to a rabbi.

"Where should I begin?" he asked.

"With the Talmud," the rabbi replied.

"How long will my studies take?"

The rabbi grew thoughtful. "Five years, no more than that."

"And then what?"

"Kabbala."

"For a long time?"

"Five years."

"And then what?"

"You'll come to me. We'll talk."

This was not a serious proposition for a man who was supposed to save the revolution. Especially for an American, who received everything in an abbreviated version, easily dissolvable like instant coffee.

Samuel Kerner and his friends went to San Francisco. They rented a rundown house in Chinatown. They slept in sleeping bags, washed with cold water, and ate once a day, in the afternoon, always the same thing: cabbage and rice. Under the guidance of Du Lun, a Chinese from Manchuria, they meditated and discussed Buddhism.

Du Lun did not require that they study for ten years. They could sit down and immerse themselves in meditation without lengthy preparations.

There were thirty Jews in Samuel's group. Their parents had been born in the States, but their grandparents' brothers and sisters, and the children of those brothers and sisters, had stayed in Europe and perished in the gas chambers.

They asked Du Lun why God had allowed Treblinka.

Du Lun did not know and asked them to meditate more deeply, with more concentration.

They meditated for ten, twelve hours at a time. The God who had permitted the Holocaust preoccupied them more than the coming world revolution.

In the following year Samuel Kerner went to Taiwan, then to South Korea, then to Macao. He became a Buddhist monk. He donned a cloth robe and settled into a small wooden cabin in the Montana mountains. He read, he thought, he listened to the falling snow. Would he hear the answer that Du Lun, the Chinese from Manchuria, did not know? Perhaps, when the heart and mind are at peace, man does not ask questions?

Samuel Kerner finished his story. He sank into thought. Suddenly he bent down and reached under the bed. He pulled out a laptop computer, placed it on his plaster knees, and started searching for something. He stared at the screen. I thought he was looking for answers, for the most important ones, but it was only a Jewish calendar for the year 5754.

It's Hanukkah!" he exclaimed. "I had a feeling that tonight is the first candle!"

He asked me to take down the Hanukkah menorah from his shelf; he lit a candle, the first one on the right, and recited the blessing.

4

American rabbis became anxious when educated, good Jewish children began to abandon their parents' homes for Chinese slums and Buddhist masters.

"If we reject these youth, we will lose the most sensitive, most profoundly spiritual people of our age," wrote Zalman Schachter, a theologian, an American, born in Żółkiewka, Poland. He decided to address the young rebels. He wanted to inform them that everything they were seeking in Buddhism could be found in Jewish tradition. He began his first lecture with the following statement: "Over two hundred years ago, in Podole, the Baal Shem Tov, the Master of the Good Name, created a movement called Hasidism. Many paths lead to God, the Baal Shem Tov taught, and God's desire is to be served in all ways. Let us not interfere with people in their service."

Rabbi Schachter devoted later meetings to the masters of Hasidism—Nachman of Bratzlav, Zusia of Annopol, Mendel of Kotzk. He published several books. He won thousands of followers. For the generation of the Age of Aquarius he became a contemporary Jewish guru.

The path to God along which he conducted the rebel Jews from Philadelphia and San Francisco led through Leżajsk, Kotzk, and Izbica Lubelska.

5

Samuel Kerner returned to the world from his mountain seclusion to help those who suffer. He settled in Boston, in the Back Bay, a district of drug addicts, homosexuals, students, and underappreciated artists.

He helped sufferers through Chinese methods: by touch, herbs, and acupuncture.

Healing through touch is based on drawing out memory. Memory is concealed in the human body, in muscle tissue. It is uncovered by touching the head, the back of the neck, the feet. Things that have been shoved deep into non-memory are recalled anew and lose the power to torment.

Usually, Samuel freed neurotic Americans from the nightmares of childhood. A German who suffered from headaches turned out to have been a submarine commander during the Second World War. The boat had sunk along with its crew; the commander survived. Samuel considered whether he should cure that German. He decided he should, because the German who had lost his crew was a man in pain.

One day Adam S. came to Samuel Kerner. He said that his brother, who had perished in the ghetto, was inhabiting him. He asked Samuel Kerner if he could help him.

The monk was confused. Adam S. had been born after the boy's death; memories of the war did not exist in him. It made no sense to look in his muscle tissue, yet he placed the patient on his couch. He began to massage the back of his neck. Nothing happened. He started repeating that he was only able to set deposited memory into motion, but he didn't finish his sentence. Adam S. burst out crying and screaming. A moment before, both had been conversing in English, but now Adam S. was shouting something in an unknown language, full of sibilant consonants.

Samuel listened in astonishment. Adam S. was clearly calling for someone in a pitiful child's voice. Then he grew furious. Then he began to be frightened. There was no doubt about it: a third person had appeared in the room. He would grow quiet for a few minutes, then turn violent like a struggling, wild little beast.

Samuel remembered what he had heard in Taiwan about people who die suddenly or from a violent death. They don't know that they have died. Their souls are unable to break their ties with earth. Chinese Buddhism is a folk religion, and folk beliefs are populated with spirits. The Chinese try to help those who are unable to leave. They show them the way.

Samuel Kerner showed the way to Adam S.'s brother.

He said, "Go to the light."

He did not understand why he was saying that, but he was certain that those were the right words.

The one who was with them, who was only wind and fear, began to follow the words.

And then Adam S. said something in that sibilant language.

The other one stopped. He turned back and moved hurriedly toward Adam.

A sudden silence descended in the room.

"What did you say to him?" Samuel asked.

"I told him, 'Don't go away,'" Adam S. replied, in his own voice again and in English.

"So you want him to remain with you?"

"After all, he's my brother," Adam S. whispered.

6

Eight months before I saw him an automobile had crushed both of Samuel's legs. The doctors said he would learn to walk in two years. He went for intensive therapy sessions every day, and after he got back I would sit on his bed and torment him with questions.

"Do you understand anything about this?"

"No. And I don't try to. The Chinese say, 'Respect the spirits, but keep them at a distance.' I did not summon Adam S.'s brother. I only gave him his voice; I made it possible for him to be heard."

"Is this at all connected with God?"

"I don't know. Everything is unclear and difficult with the God of Judaism. The Buddhist god seems easier, less imposing, and I don't worry about him. It's he who is supposed to worry about me. My task is concern for people who are suffering, not concern for a suffering God."

We broke off our conversations whenever Samuel's voice showed signs of hoarseness. The first time, I thought he was hoarse because of a cold, but he explained that it was a tumor. They had cut out only half of it; it was not cancerous. The other half, which the doctors weren't certain about, still had to be removed.

When he felt worn out, he would pick up his flutes. I would say something, and he would reply on the flute. The Indians' cedar instrument didn't know cheerful sounds, so the little room would grow sadder and sadder, more and more primordial. Finally, Samuel would order a taxi for me (women don't walk along the dark streets of the Back Bay by themselves) and I would go home.

Late one evening Adam S. phoned me from the West Coast.

He told me about his day. He had finished a paper, given an exam to his students, his son was fine, everything was fine, only he had woken up again at three and lain awake till morning.

The men in his family died young, all of them from heart attacks. That's not good. It meant he had no more than ten years left. Then what?

"You shouldn't have called him back," I said. I understood who was on his mind when he asked, "Then what?" "He would have gone to the light, wherever it is. He would have forgotten."

"I know," Adam S. agreed. "But when he began to go . . . When he was walking away like that, I felt . . . I don't know how to say this in Polish . . . I felt such *rachmones* . . ."

"Litość taką, such pity."

"Oy, I felt such *rachmones*, such intense *rachmones*, when he was leaving this world."

7

He wakes up at three and lies awake until morning.

"You're not sleeping?" his wife asks, and sits on the bed.

"I know," says Adam S., anticipating her words. "I should go . . ."

"He wants to help you," says his wife, and starts crying.

"During my last visit he told me to draw the ghetto wall and the Aryan side. He gave me a pen and paper, and said, 'Draw it for me; I don't understand what you're saying.'"

"Why should he understand?" says Adam S.'s wife, who was born in Brooklyn, just like their psychiatrist. "Explain it to him; it's not something bad. When he understands, he'll try to help you."

"Try to sleep," Adam S. says, gets dressed, and leaves the house.

He runs between the dark, slumbering gardens of his fellow professors.

The YMCA opens at six. He heads to the club and works out on the machines. He focuses on cardiovascular training.

With his graying hair, he looks more and more like his father. Less and less like that other one imprisoned inside him, untouched by death, a six-year-old forever.

The Chair

1

I told a friend of mine from Jerusalem, who is a soldier and a poet, about the crying dybbuk.

Every Jewish survivor listens with some impatience to other people's stories.

A Jewish survivor himself knows of events that are a hundred times more interesting.

"Are you finished?" he'll ask. "Now I'll tell you a better story."

So I told him about the dybbuk.

"Are you finished?" the soldier-poet asked. "Now I'll tell you . . ."

The "better story" was about Grandpa Maier and Grandma Mina. They lived in Sędziszów. The family was well-to-do and respected; Grandpa Maier held the post of mayor for a while. Later, he went into business, built a sawmill, bought up forests, and produced railroad ties. Then he moved to Podole and was a representative of the Okocim brewery. He returned to his native region shortly before the war.

Grandma Mina had pain in her legs. No one knew what was causing this even though Grandpa took her to the best doctors in Lwów. At first, Grandma limped; then she had to use a cane and walking became more and more of an effort, until finally she stopped walking entirely. Grandpa drove to Lwów and brought back a chair. It had a high back, a comfortable footrest, and was upholstered in a dark-green velvet with somewhat lighter stripes. Grandma Mina settled into the chair, rested her feet on the footrest, and heaved a great sigh.

"Now I won't stand up for the rest of my life."

From that moment, Grandma ran the house from the height of her chair. She resided in the dining room, but she knew that the fish could use more pepper and the borscht needed sugar, that her grandsons should be sitting down to their books, and the maid ought to pick up cough medicine at the pharmacy.

The medicine was gulped down by Grandpa Maier. He was given a thorough examination and problems with his lungs, thyroid, and larynx were ruled out, but he did not stop coughing.

Life went on in its normal routines: business, children, the maid, the house, except that Grandpa coughed and Grandma sat in her armchair.

When the war began, Grandpa quickly understood what was coming. He invited his Polish neighbor, a friend of the family, and the two of them locked themselves up in a room. Soon the friendly Pole began building a bunker. The work, carried out with due respect for caution, lasted a year. The shelter turned out to be spacious; it was outfitted with essential furnishings, a stock of food, even Grandma's carpet, and, naturally, the green chair.

When the decree about the ghettos was announced, Grandma and Grandpa moved into the hideout. They invited other Jewish families; a dozen or so people settled in to the bunker.

Life went on almost normally.

The friendly Pole did the shopping for them, Grandma sat in her chair, and Grandpa coughed. That cough began to disturb the bunker's tenants.

"Maier," they said. "People will hear you. Can't you control it? Is this an appropriate time for your coughing?"

Grandpa knew that it wasn't an appropriate time; the friendly Pole kept bringing new medicines, Grandma concocted *gogol-mogols*, but Grandpa did not stop coughing.

And one day the tenants in the bunker lost their patience.

And they strangled Grandpa.

And a strange thing happened.

Grandma got back the strength in her legs.

She got up from the chair.

She closed Grandpa's eyes.

She walked out of the bunker.

She knocked on the door of the friendly Pole.

"Run away," she said. "The Germans will be here in a moment."

She stopped a wagon on the road and told the driver to take her to the police station.

The Germans shot all the Jews.

They shot Grandma, too, but at the end. As a reward, they explained. Thanks to them she saw her husband's murderers die.

My acquaintance, the soldier and poet, survived the war in Kraków. The story of his Grandpa Maier and Grandma Mina was told to him after the war by the Pole who befriended his grandparents.

2

"Sędziszów," sighed the New York rabbi Haskiel Besser. "I was thinking about Sędziszów not long ago. We were driving in a sleigh through Chamonix; the driver covered our legs with a sheepskin. I caught the odor of the sheepskin and told my wife, 'I know that smell from somewhere.' In our hotel room we sat down near the open window and looked at the mountains, at the Alps. It began snowing. I told my wife, 'Now I know . . .'

"I was traveling by sleigh to Krynica, it was snowing, the driver gave us a sheepskin for our legs. A fat *grande dame* was seated beside me and she didn't stop talking. She talked about her family and her neighbors, about funerals, about someone's wedding, and all of them were from Sędziszów. Her surname was Zylberman. I don't remember her first name. Snowflakes were settling on my eyelashes, the wind was blowing, I pulled up the sheepskin and smelled the sharp odor of raw wool backed with coarse, threadbare cloth. Zylberman expressed surprise that I was cold and asked me my name.

"'Chaskiel? Just like my brother.'" And she began telling me about his successes in school. I had always spent the winter in Piwniczna, but my sister had gotten married that year and I wanted to be with her. In Chamonix I kept thinking about Piwniczna, Krynica and Sędziszów, where I have never been.

3

Had this happened in one of Isaac Bashevis Singer's stories, the fat *grande dame* in the sleigh would have known thrilling stories about people from Sędziszów. She would certainly have heard about Grandpa Maier and Grandma

Mina, whose fate had become a local legend carefully repeated from mouth to mouth. But it was snowing and the sleigh was moving, and Zylberman was talking about long ago, before everything. The green chair was still in the dining room, Grandpa was coughing peacefully, and there was no story.

Had this happened in Singer, an Aunt Yentl, the one in the little hat decorated with beads and ribbons (yellow, red, green, and white), might have told the story about Grandma Mina and Grandpa Maier. She adored strange and marvelous adventures: about a priest who lit black candles and lived with a demon-woman, red-haired Dasha, who was in love with a brute who whipped her . . . They were the most horrible experiences Aunt Yentl had ever heard of. Singer never wrote about Grandma Mina, who was the last to die, as a reward. He was afraid of the Holocaust. Even his unclean spirits, demons, dybbuks, vampires, and devils were afraid. They never ventured into a carpeted hell with a green velvet chair in a place of honor.

A Fox

The two of us women were staying in a *pension* and would pass the time by going on easy walks. We'd stroll alongside the Świder River, which was somewhat wider and deeper than usual that spring. We left immediately after breakfast; we wanted to get out before the drunks woke up around noon. They'd be lying about in the nearby woods, surrounded by empty beer cans, jars that had held their snacks, bits of string and plastic wrap.

Pani Miecia seemed not to see the trash. Through the blue eyes of a gentle child she saw gardens, flowers, and wicker armchairs.

"The veranda was over there," she said, "on the left. We

used to play poker on it. Would you believe that I once won all the money Henryk Kuna, the sculptor, staked?"

The veranda had been a feature of Mrs. Szychowa's *pension* seventy years ago, but Pani Miecia came back to these parts every year. In Świder, she had played poker with the sculptor, Kuna; in Śródborów, she had played pinochle with Duracz, the attorney; for New Year's Eve they would travel to Otwock to be with the Góreckis. True, they charged twenty-five zlotys a day, which was five times more than other proprietors did, but they served French sardines and partridges in oranges.

Every couple of days Pani Miecia was visited by her husband, Pan Waldemar. He would drop by for only a little while, because he was still in business. Lately, he had been thinking a lot about baby carriages. He had read that five hundred thousand babies are born annually in Poland, but very few baby carriages are being manufactured. One could import them from Taiwan and sell them for two million and more.

Pan Waldemar had learned economic thought in his youth, from a commercial attaché in the French Embassy. He must have been a quick study, because when the attaché went on a hunting trip to Mexico he entrusted the administration of the entire bureau to Pan Waldemar.

Pan Waldemar was supposed to have married a different woman, namely, Antonina Wajman. Her father owned shares in sixteen sugar refineries and drove a Citröen with such a fabulous suspension that you felt as if you were in a cradle. The wedding date was set; a dinner at the Hotel Europejski and tickets for a honeymoon trip to Seville had been ordered, but Antonina's brother came home from Oxford. He took a close look at the groom and said three words to his sister: "I don't advise . . ." She listened to him. The brother committed suicide immediately after the German invasion. Antonina was arrested on the Aryan side. Despite her Semitic beauty she hadn't accepted that there was a war on. She had not moved to the ghetto. She did not want to hide. She was taken away from the Simon & Stecki Restaurant; someone, no one knows who, had called the police.

Six months after the marriage that didn't take place Pan Waldemar went on vacation and noticed Miecia at a dance hall in Jastarnia.

When I made their acquaintance, at the *pension* in Świder, they had been married for fifty-seven years.

I liked going to their room for English tea and Pani Miecia's stories, which were always pleasant and ended on an unanticipated note.

"We had spent New Year's Eve in Otwock," she began one afternoon. "We had danced all night long and on New Year's Day until dinner; Waldzio left for home only in the evening, and I stayed on. It was snowing on Three Kings' Day. In a couple of hours there were huge drifts, the tracks were covered with snow, and we were cut off from the world. Do you know what my husband did? He came by sleigh from Warsaw to comfort me. 'I'm managing fine

on my own, darling,' he said. 'Stay here and relax.' So I
stayed and relaxed until an acquaintance of mine, a waitress at the Frigate, phoned. 'You're having such a pleasant rest in Otwock? In the meantime, that husband of
yours, the engineer, has been coming here every evening
all week, and always with the same woman.' I ordered a
sleigh. I caught the train in Falenica; in Warsaw I went to
my hairdresser. You should know, Miss," Pani Miecia
added in a didactic tone of voice, "in such situations a
woman must have clean, well-coiffed hair. I phoned his
office and uttered five words, very calmly, 'I'm waiting at
the Frigate.'"

Pan Waldemar was clearly off somewhere in memory
as he listened to his wife. He reached into his briefcase
and extracted a photograph. It showed a young man in
plaid plus-fours, with self-assured, seductively half-closed
eyes. "That's me," he said. "In those days. Do you find
me attractive?"

"Very much," I admitted. "But how did that conversation in the café end?"

"With a brand new fox," Pani Miecia laughed. "From
Apfelbaum's. Do you know who he was? Maurycy
Apfelbaum, 25 Marszałkowska Avenue—the most elegant
furrier in Warsaw. A marvelous silver fox; when I flung it
across my shoulder it trailed down my back to my ankles."

"From Chowańczak," Pan Waldeman interjected, and
propped the photograph of the man in plus-fours against
the sugar bowl.

"From Apfelbaum, darling," Pani Miecia insisted. "You know that no one had lovelier foxes."

"Miecia. From Chowańczak. Apfelbaum was dead by then."

"You know . . . ," she considered this, "you're right. Apfelbaum had been dead for a long time by then."

I realized then that all the stories they had told me— the romances, the betrayals, the snowdrifts, the fox—had happened during the Second World War.

For quite some time I was affected by this realization.

In the summer, Pani Miecia fell ill. Even in the hospital she had gentle, trusting eyes; she talked about the *pension* she had discovered in Międzylesie and vowed that we would go there as soon as she felt better.

I telephoned in the autumn.

"So you don't know what she did to me?!" I heard a clear note of irritation in Pan Waldemar's voice. "She died! She died on me!"

"And I told her," he said in despair, when I visited him, "let's move to Tahiti. In 1939, in *Le Matin*, a French bank was advertising a guaranteed lifetime annuity in Tahiti for 8,000 zlotys. I begged her, 'Miecia, let's sell everything. Let's go. The temperature is never above 25 degrees centigrade there, summer and winter, night and day.' And do you know what she answered me? 'And will Mrs. Szychowa move her *pension* there? And what about snow? New Year's Eve without snow?!' So we didn't go. And now she's died on me. . . ."

"The French bank guaranteed immortality in Tahiti?" I asked, but Pan Waldemar didn't hear me. He stood up. He led me to his wife's room and opened the wardrobe.

I know. It sounds unbelievable, but Pan Waldemar took out a stole made of silver fox.

"My wife asked me to . . . ," he said. "Please take it as a memento."

"I would prefer something from Apfelbaum's," I confessed. "After all, you know that no one had more beautiful foxes . . . ," and I quickly hung up the stole, afraid that Pan Waldemar would tell me where they bought it, in the Wola department store, for example, and that he would ruin my punch line.

The Tree

1

An old, bearded Jew, wearing a black hat and a long black coat, leaves his house before eight o'clock and boards the trolley on Targowa Street, near the Różycki Bazaar.

It happens sometimes that, two stops later, at Jagiellońska Street, another old Jew boards the same trolley, but as a rule they take different trolleys.

A third old Jew, who is supposed to get on two stops before the bazaar, at Zamoyski Street, is very weak and goes to the synagogue only on Saturdays.

In the synagogue they say the morning prayer, after which they eat a free kosher meal.

They return home and go to bed. They gather strength. They have to get up at three and go to the trolley. They have two prayers to say, the morning and the evening prayer.

On Saturdays, if it's not slippery outside, if it's not raining, and if there's not a strong wind, about twenty of them pray.

They are the last East European Jews in Warsaw, maybe even in Poland, and maybe even in the entire world.

2

They cling to a couple of streets in the Praga district, near the preschool. The preschool has a playground with swings and a small platform to which one ascends on stone stairs. A round synagogue once stood here, the oldest in Warsaw.[1] Modest, unadorned, it was one of the first round synagogues in Europe. It was burned out during the war; after the war, the walls were taken down. The stairs lead nowhere.

The property belonged to the Bergsons, whose forebear was King Stanisław August's banker, Szmul Zbytkower. His son, Berek, donated it to the Jewish community as a gift. "All the buildings and squares from the depths of the earth to the limit of the sky I give as an eternal gift, unso-

1. Bergman, Eleonora. "Okrągła synagoga na rogu Szerokiej i Jagiellońskiej." Typescript.

licited, of my own volition, not liable to revocation in future," he wrote in the deed of gift in 1807. "My wife and mistress, if only she were still alive!, supported me in this matter. I raise my prayers to God in the highest, that day and night His eyes may be turned toward this house."

Berek's sons requested that vice-regent Zajączek grant them permission to live in Warsaw on a street of their choosing outside the Jewish quarter, even though they wore Jewish attire and had beards. The vice-regent supported their request and presented it to Alexander I. The tsar expressed his agreement as to the street, beard, and Orthodox attire for the oldest of the brothers only.

The youngest, Michał, emigrated to Paris. He was a student of Chopin's, a composer and pianist. He composed operas and pieces for the piano.

Michał's son, Henri Bergson, was the French philosopher and Nobel laureate.[2] He wrote about the roles of instinct, intellect, and intuition. After France was occupied by the Germans, the Vichy government advised him that he would not be subject to anti-Jewish restrictions. In response, Bergson renounced the distinctions with which France had honored him and, octogenarian that he was, stood in line for many hours. In conformity with the orders of the authorities, he inscribed his name in the registry of Jews. He died soon afterward. He was close to Catholicism. He did not accept baptism. "I wished to remain

2. Weksler-Waszkinel, Romuald J. "Antysemityzm? Refleksja nad testamentem Bergsona." Typescript.

with those who will be persecuted tomorrow," he wrote in his last testament.

Two buildings are part of the property above which hover the spirits of bankers, artists, and philosophers. One is a one-story, modest building of red brick, intended once upon a time as a *mikva*, a ritual bath; the East European Jew who boards the tram at Jagiellońska Street lives there. The other is a multistory, grand building that has replaced the former asylum for beggars, wanderers, and reformed sinners. A plaque informs us that the Michał Bergson Instructional Facility of the Warsaw Community of Orthodox Believers is located in this new building. One of the apartments is occupied by an East European Jewish woman who doesn't go to synagogue on any trolley.

3

She was given the name Ninel. N-i-n-e-l, Lenin spelled backward. Her older sister was presented with the name Rema, an acronym from a Soviet slogan of the twenties: *Revoliutsiia plius Elektrifikatsiia Mira*, which means, "Revolution Plus Electrification of the World."

Rema emigrated from Poland and Ninel remained all alone with her name. She was asked about it by clerks in the Bureau of Civil Records, by postmen, the midwife, and acquaintances at summer resorts. "Ninel?" and they'd pause, while she would feverishly consider whether she should lie or assume this burden one more time with mournful dignity?

When she was fifty she went to Israel and learned that *nin-el* is a fusion of the Hebrew words for great-grandchild and God.

The day that she stopped being Lenin and became the great-granddaughter of God was one of the happiest days of her life.

Ninel's grandfather, a carter who drove someone else's horse, and her father, a journeyman tailor, came from Święciany. Her grandmother had died young and on her deathbed had called for her son, the future father of Ninel. She was no longer alive when he arrived at the hospital. The nurse wanted to show her to the boy, took him to the morgue, and got the boxes mixed up. He opened one of them and they saw a pile of amputated human hands and feet. The boy returned home, lay down, and fell asleep. He slept for several days. The doctor was called. He didn't know what to do, but he said it was an interesting case and he would happily purchase a patient in a coma. Grandfather agreed. The doctor left him money, gathered up the future father of Ninel, and grandfather bought himself a horse. The future father slept for twenty-three days, after which he woke up in amazing good health. The doctor wrote up "The Case of Patient K.," and one can find it to this day in certain reference books.

The future father of Ninel became a communist. He emigrated to Moscow. He graduated with a degree in

Marxist philosophy and then taught the subject himself.
He brought over his siblings from Święciany, Abram and
Rachela. They were all arrested in 1937. The father was in
prison for nine years, and both Rachela and Abram for
eighteen years.

They returned to Poland. Ninel graduated with a degree
in electronics. She is an expert in Jewish customs and
Talmudic law. Her son studied Hebrew and learned Jewish prayers. He was bar mitzvah at age thirteen. From then
on he had the right to put on a tallith, to pray with the
adult men, and to read aloud from the Torah in the synagogue. It was the first bar mitzvah in the Warsaw synagogue since the end of the war.

4

The East European Jew who lives in the one-story house
had a pious father who was a councilman in Łaskarzew.
He had three brothers and three sisters. He had two children and a wife. He had a horse, a wagon with a tarpaulin
for a cover, and a shop that he co-owned with his brother.
His name was Srul.

He dealt in cattle and meat—in Izdebno, Leokadia,
Zygmunty, Melanów, Chotyń, and Wielki Las.

The peasants with whom he had done business and to
whom he had loaned money (he would say "Open the

drawer, take as much as you need, and pay me back when you can") decided that he had to survive.

They gave him the name Zygmunt.

They allowed him to spend the nights in their barns, woods, and haystacks. They fed him bread, soup, and potatoes. When his wife Jochwed and his daughter Basia died in the ghetto, they told him that he had to live for his son. When Szmulek died, they said he had to live for them.

He survived thanks to the peasants of Izdebno, Leokadia, Zygmunty, Melanów, Chotyń, and Wielki Las.

After the war, he went to the Office of State Security; he testified that a certain Home Army prisoner had not killed Jews.

He went to factories and said, "This girl's father saved me, and you don't want to hire her?"

He arranged for them to get invitations to go abroad. He sold them meat from his kosher butcher stall without a ration card and gave them calves' feet and veal for free. He was a guest at their family parties. He danced with other men's fiancées at other men's weddings and sat at the table near the parish priest and the village headman.

In the one-story house over which hover the spirits of bankers, artists and philosophers, in a room that used to be the bath-house dressing room, the East European Jew looks at holiday greeting cards. They come, as they do every year, from Izdebno, Leokadia, Zygmunty, Melanów, Chotyń, and Wielki Las.

Finally, he reaches for an envelope from New York.

"Read it aloud," he says. "I'm almost blind."

The envelope has been cut open. The thin airmail paper, covered with awkward writing, has been read many times.

"Reading your letter, I wept bitterly. I, too, regret that I ran away from the train. Life is lonely. I wish you good health, Your Mojsze."

They were traveling in the same freight car to Treblinka: Mojsze Landsman, a friend from Łaskarzew, and he with his four-year-old son. When the son smothered to death in the freight car, Mojsze Landsman whispered, "Now," and jumped first.

"Write," he says to me. "I'm almost blind."

He hands me note paper and starts dictating:

"Dear Mojsze, you are right. For whom did we jump? Why the hell did we jump? Did we have to jump from that train?"

But no . . .

He has changed his mind. He takes the paper away from me and hands me a shiny card. It is a picture of a Christmas tree with a lot of colored lights and burning candles.

"Write," he says. "Dear Mojsze, on the occasion of New Year's Day 1995 I wish you much health and . . ."

"And . . . ?"

"Well, write, write. Don't you know what you're supposed to wish people for the New Year?"

5

The son of Ninel, God's great-granddaughter, was prepared for his bar mitzvah by the bearded Jew who boards the trolley on Targowa Street.

He was a *shochet*, a ritual slaughterer. He was taught the art of slaughtering by Izaak Dublin, while Mosze Tipnis taught him Talmud—both of them the most pious, the most learned Jews in all Rokitno.

When you have reached sixty years of age you can no longer be a slaughterer. Your hand might tremble, the knife would wound the animal, and the meat would be *treyf*.

When the Jew from Targowa Street stopped being a *shochet*, the last one in Warsaw, the last one in Poland, he decided to emigrate to Israel.

He got his furniture ready for the journey, locked it up in one room, hung a padlock on the door, and hid the key in a linen pouch. He moved into the kitchen. Pots that there's no point in washing, jars that should be recycled, stale baked goods, old newspapers, pieces of aluminum foil, old shoes, bottle caps, corks, and rags all piled up.

When he comes back from morning prayer he takes off his black suit and lies down in his underwear on the bed, which there's no point in making up with fresh linen. He stretches out his white beard and grayish-yellow bare arms on the grayish-yellow comforter. He sinks into a short, alert sleep before his afternoon prayer.

He would like to sail to Haifa on a freighter with his furniture. He would like to travel free of charge, so he visits the Israeli Embassy and asks for a ticket.

They reply that that is impossible.

A couple of years pass. He visits the Embassy, asks for a ticket.

They say it's impossible.

A couple of years pass.

Maybe in other countries, in West European countries, one GOES to Israel.

An East European Jew does not simply GO, just like that.

HE PREPARES TO LEAVE—and that must go on and on.

The bearded man from Targowa Street, the last Polish *shochet*, has been preparing to leave for Israel for thirty years.

6

A middle-aged Jew came to visit the last *shochet*. Also an East European Jew, but from Wola.

His father had a tailor's shop on the corner of Redutowa and Wolska Streets, opposite the well.

Water was carried in buckets on yokes.

The well pump was red.

His father made suits.

The wife of factory-owner Krygier paid him 115 zlotys to sew her a woolen suit.

His father bought a wringer for five zlotys, a washtub for fifteen, and gambled away the rest at cards.

This happened right before the Passover holiday. His mother sent the children to the rabbi. The rabbi also lived on Wolska Street, across from the *cheder*. All five of the children went there, he and his sisters Krajndł, Frendł, Fajge, and Hania. The rabbi gave them four dozen eggs and a packet of fat from the Central Agricultural Co-op.

He watched his father carefully, looking at how he played and how he lost, and he drew a conclusion: in all card games, it is possible to give fate a helping hand.

His parents were deaf mutes. They spoke to each other in Yiddish, using sign language. Thanks to that circumstance he did not have a Jewish accent and after the liquidation of the ghetto he was able to pose as an Aryan kid without much difficulty.

He was a street singer, a shoeshine boy, a cigarette seller, a cowherd, and a railway workers' assistant. He lived at the West Station, on platform four, in the comptroller's booth. German troop trains passed through the station carrying soldiers on leave from the Eastern front. People bought champagne and sardines from the soldiers on the trains and sold them flashlights, batteries, and fountain pens. He traded at night; first thing each morning he turned the goods into cash at Hala Mirowska, and during the day he walked around with a hammer and checked the rails, wheels, and brakes.

He married a Polish woman. She bore him sons who did not want to be Jews.

He doesn't like to brag, but there is no better player than he in the Marriott Hotel or the Rio Grande Club, nor in the Różycki bazaar. He plays poker, roulette, and sixty-six. He wouldn't want to brag, but there is no better gambler in all Warsaw.

And it all comes from the fact that his father gambled away his earnings from the suit he'd made for the wife of Krygier the factory owner.

The last gambler came to see the last *shochet* about a delicate matter.

He has a woman, Tośka. She is easygoing, with a large bosom and kind, blue eyes. His wish is that Tośka should turn out to be Jewish.

Once, she was telling him about how her father would kill a rooster: "'Slash . . . ,' and he'd make a smooth motion across his throat, and then the rooster was dead."

A sudden hope dawned in the gambler.

He and Tośka went to see the last *shochet*.

They put him in their car.

They drove to the countryside.

They bought a rooster.

The last *shochet* plucked a few feathers from the rooster's neck. He removed his ritual knife—slender and sharp, with no nicks in it—from its linen sheath. He checked with his finger to be sure the blade was smooth. With a single motion he drew it across the throat: "Slash . . ."

They looked at Tośka.

"Is that how your father did it?"

"Yes," she agreed.

"Then he was a Jew," the last gambler rejoiced. "Maybe he was even a butcher?"

"Did he check the gullet?" the last *shochet* asked anxiously, carefully examining the killed bird. "There cannot be even a grain of feed remaining in the gullet; a bird with feed is unclean."

Tośka could not remember if her father used to check the gullet, but the last gambler was not interested in details.

"Your father was a Jew, you are a Jew, at last your life's pathways are straightened out, and it's all thanks to me."

He took her to the synagogue, sent her to the women's balcony, stood beside the Torah and prayed, as he did every Saturday, for the souls of his four sisters: Krajndł, Frendł, Fajge, and Hania.

7

The last cantor, Dawid B., and his wife, Zysla, decided to emigrate for the sake of their son.

The son had passed his high school graduation exam; he earned 5's in all his science exams and he wanted to study electronics.

Dawid and Zysla yearned for him to graduate from college, to find a Jewish girl, and for the girl to bear him nice children. They yearned for a peaceful, happy old age spent near their children and grandchildren.

Everything was prepared for their emigration.

They had the down comforter restored. (The proprietress of the workshop on Wileńska Street had never seen such down, so they explained to her that it was from pigeons. Miriam, Zysla's mother, had sent the comforter to them in Łuck literally at the last minute and it was the only thing that they had not exchanged for flour and potatoes. Thanks to the comforter they survived the wartime freezing weather in the Komi Autonomous Soviet Socialist Republic and in Akmolińska oblast.)

They placed the comforter in a chest along with a clock that chimed every quarter hour. It was an unusual clock. Dawid B. had replaced the numbers of the beautiful, old clockface with Hebrew letters. Now, instead of 1 there was *aleph*, instead of 2, *beys*, instead of 3, *gimel*, and so on. (His father taught him singing and his love of clocks. He was the owner of a clock-maker's shop in the center of Kielce, and also the cantor in a small synagogue on Nowowarszawska Street.)

They packed up their pictures. A certain Shevchenko, a Ukrainian, had painted them. Everyone ordered paintings before leaving. They represented women standing above the Sabbath candles, men studying Torah, and Jews as eternal wanderers. They liked the scenes with the Torah because the synagogue reminded them of the one in Kielce, on Nowowarszawska Street, but they had reservations about the wandering Jew. He was sitting there exhausted, barefoot, beside a road that ran through a field, with the Holy Book in one hand, a walking stick in the other, his shoes slung over his shoulders. Maybe they were too tight; maybe he didn't want to wear them out. That was it: there was a serious mistake in those shoes—they were old, dirty, and they touched the book. (Zysla pointed this out. She knew the prohibitions and commandments perfectly, because she had been taught religion by the wife of the Powiśle rabbi. The rabbi lived on the corner of Chełmska Street and Zysla lived on Czerniakowska; there was a *mikva* across the street and a prayer house. After the rabbi's death his son-in-law, a follower of the Piaseczno *tzaddik*, inherited the position. He had a medical diploma, and in addition he was the very own brother-in-law of the Kozienice *tzaddik*. When Zysla was in the hospital, the rabbi gave her mother medicine and uttered three words: *Got zol trefn*, God will help. And God did help; the next day, her fever broke.)

They gave away their furniture.

They sold the piano.

They packed up their clothing.

Zysla tidied up the apartment and went downstairs to take out the garbage.

When she returned the window was wide open. Someone was screaming in the courtyard, horrendous screams.

The cantor's wife wants to believe in an unhappy accident. The women in the synagogue believe in an unhappy love.

The photograph on the headstone, in the Jewish cemetery, portrays a good-looking boy with serious, dark eyes.

The pictures on the apartment walls portray women praying over Sabbath candles, men studying Torah, and the wandering Jew.

On the bed there's a comforter made of pigeon down.

The clock strikes every quarter hour.

Two large suitcases stand in the main room. In them is the son's clothing, packed for the journey. They haven't opened the suitcases in twenty-five years. Every day they dust them and cover them again with a white, crocheted tablecloth.

The last cantor boards the trolley at Zamoyski Street.

He attends synagogue only on Saturdays.

He sings only once a year, on Yom Kippur.

He sings *El mole rachamim*, God full of mercy.

All year he gathers his strength for that day and that song.

All the Jews in the synagogue are waiting for it.

From his frail, old man's body emerges a voice that is clear, powerful, overflowing with love and despair.

No one sings the *El mole rachamim* anymore like the last Warsaw cantor does.

8

It is time for a question: What is meant by "East Europeans," and where does the East begin?

For Bohumil Hrabal it begins where "the Austrian, empire-style railroad stations end." That is not clear. The empire style was dominant in architecture when there were no railroads or railroad stations. Perhaps he was thinking about the later white Austrian buildings bordered with green tiles. In that case, Eastern Europe would begin east of the stations in Leżajsk, Sarzyna, and Nisko —starting only in Stalowa Wola.

For Agnieszka and Henryk Samsonowicz the East begins immediately beyond the Vistula River. On the road to Dzbądz we passed the Śląsko-Dąbrowski bridge, drove into Targowa, and Agnieszka said, "Oho, the East."

But at the corner of Kawęczyńska and Radzymińska Streets, a good five kilometers from there, in a private lending library, they had all of Proust throughout the grim 1950s. The prewar, gray-haired proprietress took the prewar volumes down from the shelf, each wrapped in packing paper, and said, "*This* you should read."

Andrzej Czajkowski, the pianist, brought Proust back from Paris. But I brought it back from a lending library on Kawęczyńska Street.

Should Eastern Europe, then, have begun in front of the lending library with all of Proust?

For Abraham J. Heschel, philosopher and theologian, the borders of the East were unimportant, because East European Jews lived in time more than in space. And if they lived in space, then it was between the abysses and heaven.[3]

According to Jewish legend, "Poland" derives from the Hebrew words *po-lin*, "reside here." Jews fleeing pogroms and the plague in Germany discovered these words written on a piece of paper. The paper came from heaven. It was lying under a tree. In the branches of the tree wandering souls were hidden. Only a pious Jew reciting the evening prayer could help them. If, therefore, there exists a boundary point for Eastern Europe, it is the tree under which that piece of paper was lying.

---

3. In his essay "Pańska jest ziemia. Świat duchowy Żydów Europy Wschodniej" [The earth is the Lord's: The spiritual world of the Jews of Eastern Europe], Abraham J. Heschel wrote about the colorfulness of the world that the East European Jews created. They had a language and literature, they had their own *tzaddiks* and bankers, learned men and artisans, socialists and Hasids, their own dishes, melodies, jokes, costumes, sighs, gestures, and manner of holding their head. They had "a touching charm" that derived from a mixture of "intellectualism and mysticism."

That world is gone. The few survivors give no suggestion of this. They bring to mind an orchestra that I once heard in Russia. It was made up of musicians who had participated in a performance of Shostakovich's *Seventh Symphony*. The composition was born in besieged Leningrad; it was played for the first time during the war. The musicians who had not perished at the front, who had not frozen to death, had not died of hunger and of old age, came together many years later and performed the symphony one more time. The conductor signaled to the orchestra and the surviving instruments responded. Sometimes only silence responded. Sometimes a lone, absurd sound could be heard. The East European Jews sound today like that crippled symphony orchestra.

Salvation

Dawid, the Lelów *tzaddik*, taught that "whosoever, whether man or nation, has not achieved awareness of his own errors, will not achieve salvation. We can be saved to the extent that we are aware of our own selves."

He had a son who also became a rabbi in Lelów. That Lelów rabbi had a son and a grandson, the rabbis of Szczekociny. The Szczekociny rabbi had a daughter named Rywka, a granddaughter named Chana, whom they called Andzia, and a great-granddaughter named Lina.

One hot July day in 1942, Chana, known as Andzia, the *tzaddik*'s granddaughter in the sixth generation, and her daughter, seven-year-old Lina, were riding through the streets of the Warsaw Ghetto to the Umschlagplatz. A few minutes earlier they had been led out of their home on Twarda Street and loaded onto a one-horse rack wagon. Two Jewish policemen were seated in it; one urged the horse on and the other watched over the people. They were old people who asked for nothing, did not pray, and did not try to run away.

The wagon turned onto Ciepła Street. The policemen were conversing in hushed tones, consulting each other. They could do one of two things: surround the next house and drive everyone out, or close off the street and conduct a lightning-fast roundup. The one who was whipping the horse was in favor of surrounding the house; the one who was in charge of the people urged him to agree to a roundup.

A man who was sitting in the wagon disrupted their consultation.

"Let them go," he said. He was thinking of Lina and her mother, Andzia.

The policemen didn't want to respond to absurd requests, but several women joined the old man.

"Let them go, they're young; let them live a little longer."

"Don't you know that I have a quota?" said the policeman who was driving the horse. "I have to deliver ten Jews to the square. The two of us together have to deliver twenty Jews. Are you going to give us someone instead of them? If you do, we'll free them."

The old folks stopped asking; the policeman's demand was as inappropriate as their request.

The wagon rolled along very slowly. People say of a horse that moves one leg after the other that it is moving at a walk, but in the ghetto such words are not used. In the meantime, the horse moved one leg after another, although it could have hurried, because there were few pedestrians on the streets.

"Everything," Andzia and Lina recalled, "was happening in silence and without haste."

"Well?" The policeman addressed them directly. "Who is going to go to the Umschlagplatz in your place? Do you have someone?"

They were approaching the spot where Ciepła Street intersected Grzybowska Street at an angle.

They drove along for a few more meters and spotted a woman. She was walking along Grzybowska. She had no intention of running away. On the contrary. She was approaching their wagon at a calm, deliberate pace. They met up with her alongside No. 36. Lina remembered this because her preschool teacher, Pani Eda, lived at No. 36.

The woman leaned her arm on the wooden shaft and said, not quite asking a question or affirming an obvious fact, "You don't want to go to the Umschlagplatz, ma'am, right?"

She was speaking to Andzia.

Andzia, taken aback, was silent.

"She doesn't want to go," someone called out, and then the woman addressed Andzia again.

"Please get down; I'll go instead of you."

Andzia and Lina still sat there, even though people were beginning to yell at them.

"What are you waiting for? Get down!"

"Get down," the policeman seated on the coachman's box echoed what the people were saying, and only then did Andzia lower her daughter to the roadway and jump down herself.

The woman clambered onto the wagon.

Both policemen were silent.

"Please give her something," someone called out to Andzia, probably the same man who was the first to ask the policeman to let her go.

Andzia quickly took off her ring and gave it to the woman.

The woman slipped the ring onto her finger. She didn't look at Andzia any more. She looked straight ahead.

Andzia and Lina returned home. Grandma Rywka was sitting there erect, stiff, holding her clasped hands on her knees. They told her about the woman. Grandma Rywka opened her hand. They saw a small vial with gray powder. "If you hadn't returned . . . ," she said. They were astounded. Grandma Rywka, the fifth-generation granddaughter of the Lelów *tzaddik*, was a pious woman. She wore a wig. When her wig was taken to the hairdresser's on Friday morning to be combed for the Sabbath, she would put on a kerchief so that no one should see her shaved head, and now she was clutching a vial of poison kept ready for a sinful, suicidal death. She was taken to the Umschlagplatz a few days later, with her grandsons and her daughter-in-law. Andzia and her daughter made it to the Aryan side and survived the war.

2

"What did that woman look like?" Lina's mother was asked whenever she told the story of the rack wagon, and she told it throughout her life.

"She was tall. She was wearing a suit. A nice, well-tailored suit made of dark-gray flannel. She had on boots, so-called officer shoes, that were popular in Warsaw during the war. I don't remember her hairdo; I think it was combed in a roll. Women used to wind their hair at the time on long wires that were turned either down or up on both sides of the face. In a word, she was an elegant woman," Lina's mother would emphasize invariably.

"Even those boots looked as if she had put them on not out of necessity, but only to look elegant."

"Maybe she knew she was going to die and so she got dressed for death?" one of the women listening to the story suggested. "People put a lot of weight on their final costume."

"She didn't look like a madwoman?" people would ask.

"No. She behaved calmly."

"Maybe she had lost someone and nothing mattered to her?"

"She didn't look as if she was in despair."

"The mess kit . . . ," Lina would prompt.

"Right. She was holding an empty mess kit."

"How do you know it was empty?"

"Because she was dangling it without any effort."

"That could have been Miriam," I said when Lina and her husband, Władek, told me about the woman. They didn't understand.

"Miriam. The one whom the Christians later referred to as Mary."

This possibility hadn't occurred to them yet; rather, they had assumed it was the *tzaddiks* who had intervened.

Władek was reminded of a wartime joke, a witticism that was repeated in the ghetto. When the Germans drove people out of the church for Jewish converts one man remained in the church—the last Jew, the one on the cross. He descended from the cross and beckoned to his Mother, "*Mame, kim . . .*" which in Yiddish means, "Mama, come . . ." And so she went to the Umschlagplatz. But wearing a suit? Not likely, because she appeared in her robe from the church images and with a halo. With an empty mess kit? There was food in it before, but she asked someone, "Is it true that you are hungry?" She fed them and went to Ciepła Street and the rack wagon.

My work as a reporter has taught me that logical stories, without riddles and holes in them, in which everything is obvious, tend to be untrue. And things that cannot be explained in any fashion really do happen. In the end, life on earth is also true, but it cannot be logically explained.

3

Dawid of Lelów's remains were buried one hundred eighty years ago in the local cemetery. The cemetery is gone, but recently the *tzaddik*'s grave was restored. Chaim Środa, the son of Josef the glazier, pointed out the spot. Dawid was resting in the community co-operative's store, in the hardware section. (After the war a warehouse and two stores—a grocery and an agricultural implements store— were built on the Jewish cemetery.) A rabbi from Jerusalem asked the director of the store to move the hardware, and Hasidim who were followers of Dawid started digging. After a couple of hours they uncovered the foundation. They found a skull, the tibias, and individual bones of the *tzaddik*'s hands. They laid down their shovels, lit candles, and said Kaddish. The rabbi arranged the remains and covered them with dirt. A couple of months later a tomb was constructed and a wall was erected to separate it from the rest of the store. On the anniversary of the *tzaddik*'s death his pupils came from around the world and left letters with requests as they used to do in former times.

Chaim Środa was born in Lelów, near the Białka River. He went to work with his father. On his back he carried frames holding panes of glass secured with belts of woven linen; in one hand, he held a can of putty, and in the other hand, a sack filled with tools. They glazed windows in Sokolniki, Nakło, and Turzyn. Every day they walked up to fifteen kilometers; they charged one zloty for each window they installed.

The Lelów Jews sold their goods at markets. In Pilica on Tuesdays, in Szczekociny on Wednesdays, in Żarki on Thursdays, but on Fridays they went only to nearby villages in order to make it back home in time for the Sabbath. On Friday mornings they carried essential items in the baskets: hair ribbons; sugar in paper sacks, each packet weighing ten dekagrams because there weren't any peasants who could afford a whole kilogram; dye for linens; and starch, also in sacks, but weighing less than the sugar. They would come back at dusk. In their baskets they now had eggs, white cheese, and bottles of milk. They washed up, changed clothes, and went to the synagogue. After the prayers they ate challah and fish. Of the eight hundred Lelów Jews, eight survived the war; one of them lives in Poland—Chaim Środa. His father, Josef the glazier, was shot in Częstochowa. His mother, Małka, née Potasz, his three brothers, Hirsz, Dawid, and Aron, and his three sisters, Ałta, Sara, and Jochwed, were sent to Treblinka.

Chaim escaped from the camp. He hid in sixteen different houses, houses in which he had installed windows before the war.

Over the grave of Dawid of Lelów, the great-great-great-grandfather of Andzia, the same conversation takes place every year.

"Our *tzaddik* taught: you will not achieve salvation if you do not recognize yourself and your errors," says the rabbi from Jerusalem, the leader of the Lelów Hasidim. "But remember, it is never too late to turn to God, blessed be His name."

"Here, there was no salvation, rabbi. Here, there was no room for any God," invariably retorts the son of Josef, the Lelów glazier—Chaim Środa.

Hamlet

1

Czajkowski, Andrzej, b. November 1, 1935, Warsaw, d. June 26, 1982, London, Pol. pianist and composer. Studied, *inter alia*, with L. Lévy, S. Szpinalski, and S. Aszkenazi (piano), K. Sikorski and N. Boulanger (comp.). 1955 eighth place in the Fifth International F. Chopin Competition in Warsaw; 1956 third place in the Queen Elizabeth Competition in Brussels. From 1956 resided abroad. Gave concerts in many countries under the dir. of, *inter alia*, K. Böhm, P. Klecki, D. Mitropoulos, F. Reiner in repertoire ranging from Bach to music of the 20th c. Made many recordings for RCA Victor and Pathé Marconi. Compositions—seven sonnets and "Ariel" inspired by Shakespeare, for voice and piano, two string quartets, two piano concertos, a piano trio, the opera *The Merchant of Venice*. . . . (From *Encyklopedia Muzyczna PWM*, Warsaw, 1987.)

2

We don't know each other.

I saw you once, a long time ago, from a great distance. You were seated at the piano, in the Philharmonic, your right profile turned toward me.

The people I used to write about I knew personally; I knew how they laughed, perspired, drummed their fingers, whom they emulated, and with whom they shared a drink. You, I have looked at in photographs. Once again you were seated at the piano, invariably displaying your right profile.

Małgorzata B. found a photograph *en face* in the archives. It had been glued onto a card with these words inscribed on it: Department of Protective Services for Orphaned Children. A Mrs. Slosberg from the city of Kimberley in South Africa sent you, an orphaned child, parcels and money. In the first quarter, three thousand zlotys, in the second another three, in the third four and a half thousand.

Not bad. An acquaintance of mine used to get that much for managing the literature department at the Czytelnik publishing house.

You were eleven years old at the time.

You had a part on the right side and big, serious eyes. A white collar was placed on your blue-black shirt, dark as soot, and a patterned handkerchief, batiste, it appears, had been tucked into your pocket.

I know those postwar photos and postwar serious eyes. An acquaintance of mine who is also a writer says that eyes like that are not the privilege of Jewish boys. Little Greek boys have almost identical eyes. A man asks them about something in a language they have never heard. They look at the man with knowing eyes and lead him, unerringly, to a shop where they can put cars on a lift to work on them.

A stupid comparison. Little Jewish boys with serious eyes indicate how to reach God, not a service station.

It is time to explain why I am writing.

Because of the case of Halina S. The woman with whom you want to have a son named Gaspard.

She sent me a letter:

"Andrzej appeared to me in a dream. He said, 'Die already, die; I am bored here without you.' I interpreted the word 'here' as interplanetary space. I imagined that the Spirit of Andrzej is circling there like an astronaut for whom there is no return to earth.

"He appeared in my dreams for the last time before my heart attack. The doctor came every day and asked me,

'Why are you getting weaker by the day?' I scrawled my will on a sheet of graph paper. I left Andrzej's letters and papers to you, Hania.

"I felt I was doing exactly what he wanted. Because although he didn't know you, you were close to him, closer perhaps than I. He read your *Shielding the Flame*.[1] That was important; it was precisely because of that book that he didn't destroy his notes.

"Now the Spirit of Andrzej will appear to you and you will give it shelter.

"Love,

"H."

So:

She left me your papers and your Spirit in her will.

Could I refuse?

Halina suspects that you are among us. She was talking about you when she suddenly turned pale and fell back onto the bed. The doctor ran an EKG and sent her to the hospital. I returned home. I was laid low with back pain.

When both of us recovered, Halina asked me, "Do you remember what we were talking about when I passed out?"

Naturally, I remembered. We were talking about your attempts at summoning a son named Gaspard to life.

"That couldn't possibly please him," Halina exclaimed. "You mustn't write about that."

Is that the truth? Do you intend to interfere with my

1. See note p. 132.

writing? The hero's spirit would be an even greater annoyance than a living hero?

An acquaintance of mine, the editor of *The Fortune Teller* magazine, assured me that the spirit was all right, but the cause of the sicknesses was Scorpio, the zodiac sign. Five planets were within Scorpio's reach at the same time. Because it is a sign of carnal love and of death, good energy, flowing toward us from the planets, was negated. That is the source of the many recent sicknesses and misfortunes, like the bursting of the hot water pipes, or flooded apartments. But the power of Scorpio is already coming to an end. On the twenty-third of November the planets will pass into the sign of Sagittarius and will send good energy.

Andrzej.

We are constructing little jokes here out of the stars, but, after all, you were born on the first of November.

You are a Scorpio!

The sign of death and carnal love!

3

One more thing, in connection with your presumed interference.

David Ferré, a middle-aged bearded guy, an American engineer with General Motors and Boeing, and also a music critic, read about the skull in the newspapers. It was July 1982. The news was reported by the Associated Press:

"André Tchaikowsky, the Polish-born pianist who died of cancer in Oxford, has willed his skull to the Royal Shakespeare Theatre."

Some newspapers wrote that all your life you had dreamed of being an actor. Others, that you loved the theater and it bothered you when Hamlet held a plastic skull in his hands.

David Ferré was touched by this news. He took leave from Boeing and flew to London to hear some music and to inquire about you. He rented a car at the airport. He looked for somewhere to stay; a rental agency recommended a house in Chelsea. He walked into the front room. A book was on the table: *My Guardian Devil: The Letters of Andrzej Czajkowski and Halina Sander*. The house in which he found himself belonged to two close friends of yours.

Conversations about you took up six years of David Ferré's life. He wrote a biographical sketch titled "The Other Tchaikowsky." When he finished it he settled in a mountain village and took up carpentry.

Thanks to him and a few other people I know a lot about you. I intend to tell you about this; you used to like stories about yourself. You would listen with interest, insisting that you don't remember your own life.

4

Your grandmother, Celina S.

She was born in the last century, in 1889. That is what is

recorded in the registry of Jews who survived. She may have been older; when replacing destroyed documents women liked to make themselves younger.

She had a daughter, Fela, and a son, Ignacy. Her husband, a doctor, came back from the First World War with syphilis. They divorced. Two admirers proposed marriage; she asked the children which one they preferred. They cried out, "Uncle Mikołaj," because he brought better candies. She married Mikołaj, the owner of a law firm, but she lived with the other man.

She was a brunette of medium height, with a short neck and light, impudent eyes. She played the harp, knew foreign languages, liked poker, and sought out strong men. She was one of the first beauticians in Poland. She founded her own school and a beauty-cream plant under French license. The firm was called Cédib. When the business starting going under, she sold half the shares to a doctor named Muszkatblat.

Your mother, Fela.

She was prettier and taller than Celina. She was her opposite: calm, pensive, lacking energy and strength. She graduated from the beauty school. She liked changing hair color. She played the piano fairly well and read a lot. She grew weary of that very quickly. She got married in Paris to a refugee from Germany, and gave birth to you a year later. She left her husband and fell in love with Albert. She was with him until the end. She died in Treblinka at the age of twenty-seven.

Your father, Karl.

He studied law in Lipsk, fled from Hitler to France. He worked in the fur business. He couldn't stand either furs or business. He wanted to be a lawyer, but France did not recognize his German diploma. He suffered bouts of depression; he was treated with electric shocks, after which he developed Parkinson's disease. It tormented him until the end of his life. He died in Paris. He saw you when you were twelve and when you were forty-five.

5

In a 1938–39 telephone book there is an S. Mikołaj, attorney, Przejazd 1, telephone 115 313. All of them lived there: Celina and her husband, her son, her daughter-in-law, her daughter, and you. They had affairs, played poker, danced the fox trot, liked lilies of the valley, sent snapshots from Ciechocinek—the men in white panama hats, the women in veils and with a swirl of hair falling over one eye. Prehistoric times. Some kind of Tertiary period, but with the useful discovery of photography.

Przejazd 1 . . .

In the same building lived a medical student, one J.S., who was in love with the singer Marysia Ajzensztadt.

In the same building lived Helena, pale and morose, the

queen of the ball in the Lwów Literary Casino, and her little daughter.

Downstairs, in the Art café, Władysław Szlengel read his poems.

Yes, the same building. Two stairwells, with an entrance on Leszno Street.

6

Celina S.'s partner, as I have said, was Dr. Muszkatblat.

His original first name was Perec; after he converted, he became Bolesław. His wife managed the Cédib firm on Three Crosses Square. Their two children were looked after by "Panna Marynia." With the savings she accumulated in the doctor's household, M. purchased a modest apartment on Sienna Street. When the children entered school she completed a course of study in tailoring with Pani Wiśniewska—the most expensive course in Warsaw (it cost 200 zlotys, not counting chalk and the paper for patterns).

The war broke out. (That was the end of prehistoric times—of harps, betrayals, the fox trot, and resorts.)

Bolesław Muszkatblat, Celina S.'s partner, swallowed potassium cyanide. His son and daughter were in a camp. Ruta Muszkatblat decided to go over to the Aryan side. She made a mistake: it was a sunny day and she dressed in a warm overcoat. A *szmalcownik*, a blackmailer, brought her to the police station.

"That will cost you four thousand," said the policeman. "We'll wait until 1:00 p.m."

Ruta M. asked them to notify Maria Ostrowska, "Panna Marynia," the children's nanny.

Maria had one thousand at hand.

It was 10:00 a.m.

She ran to her wealthiest client, the owner of a dairy store on Pańska Street. She wasn't there; she hadn't returned from her summer home.

She remembered a doctor, one of Dr. M.'s colleagues from medical school. He lived on Poznańska Street; it was the third or fourth house on the left if you approached it from Aleje Jerozolimskie.

He opened the door.

She said, "Pani Ruta is at the police station on Krochmalna. They want four thousand and I have one thousand . . ."

"I have nothing in common with Jews!" the colleague from school days shouted, and slammed the door.

She went to Anin to see an acquaintance who used to sew ball gowns before the war. It was almost twelve o'clock. She said, "I have one thousand . . ."

Her acquaintance gave her a gold ring. She asked her to pawn it, keep the receipt, and redeem it after the war.

There was no train back to Warsaw. There was no time for pawning it. Maria ran with the ring to the police station.

"You're fifteen minutes too late," said the policeman.

7

Celina's husband, the one who brought the children the better candies, died. Tactfully, in his own bed, just in time. Celina S. buried him and left the ghetto with a group of laborers who worked outside the wall. One of her former pupils gave her Aryan papers; from then on she was Janina Czajkowska. Another pupil prepared a hiding place for her. She went back for her daughter and grandson, but Fela did not want to leave.

"Just the two of you will manage to survive; as a threesome, we'll all perish."

Celina tried insisting.

"Save him," Fela repeated. "I don't have the strength; I'm going to die."

With her beautician's skill, Celina S. applied hydrogen peroxide to the boy's hair. She put a dress on him. She said goodbye to her daughter.

"Mama will come back to you in a couple of days," Fela promised.

Celina S. led the blond "girl" to the gate on Leszno Street. She held the child's hand firmly in one of her hands;

with the other, she slipped the gendarme 50 zlotys. They crossed the street and set off in the direction of Theater Square.

"Don't look up," she whispered.

They were on the Aryan side.

8

You moved in with Panna Monika. There was a wardrobe in the main room. The apartment was on the ground floor; tenants passed by your door, neighbors looked in—the safest place was inside the wardrobe. A chamber pot was placed there. You found it by touch and learned to pee without making any noise. The clothing had been taken out; in the wardrobe were darkness, the chamber pot, and you.

Every so often grandmother would visit you. You would come out of the wardrobe and Panna Monika would stand watch over the front door. Grandmother would give her money, after which she would take a bottle of hydrogen peroxide out of her bag and wet your hair where it was growing out dark. Next, she would set the liquid aside and take out a prayer book. She taught you prayers (she did not know them herself; she had to look at the book). At the end, she would drink tea and listen to the landlady's complaints about the rising cost of living and the danger your presence exposed her to. Both the one and the other were true, so grandmother would reach into her wallet again. Finally, she said goodbye, promising that she would visit you soon. She kept her word. She kept coming— with money, prayers, and hydrogen peroxide. You didn't ask her where she was living, where she was going, and where she got the money. You didn't ask why you had to sit in the wardrobe—children didn't ask stupid questions then.

Sometimes you wanted to know something about your mama.

"She's all right," your grandmother would answer. "She'll come to you in a couple of days."

A couple of days would pass.

Grandmother would say, "She was busy; don't cry."

A couple of days would pass.

You understood, finally, that your mama would never come to you and you stopped asking.

I shall tell you something now.

I knew a certain girl. She was your age; she also had dark eyes like you and hair that was bleached with hydrogen peroxide. Her mother was a beautician. You won't believe this, but her name was Fela and she graduated from the Cédib school which was founded by your grandmother.

Strange, isn't it?

I knew that little girl quite well, because I know what the Aryan side was for a child.

It was not death or fear. A five- or six-year-old child is not afraid of death.

The Aryan side was an apartment from which everyone has gone outside.

A window that you do not go near, even though no one is watching you.

A courtyard from which the echo of footsteps and someone's whistle, a melody broken off in the middle of a measure, reach you.

A wardrobe that you enter at the sound of the doorbell.

The Aryan side was loneliness and silence.

Monika was expecting a child. She was unmarried and you associated her condition with the immaculate conception. Words that you knew from the book of prayer came to life. A virgin was to bear a son. The son might become a new Christ. You were ready to throw out the chamber pot, to move over, and make room for him in the wardrobe. You fell into euphoria. You talked too much and too loudly. One day you started praying to Monika, but at the words "and blessed be the fruit of thy womb," she flew into a rage.

"You little rat!" she screamed. "Are you making fun of me?"

In vain, you explained that she had conceived like the Virgin Mary. She wouldn't stop shrieking. She summoned your grandmother. She said that you were making a lot of noise, that you were behaving shamefully; she didn't want to explain why and she demanded that you leave her home.

"We have nowhere to go," grandmother said, terrified.

"Go to the Gestapo!" Monika screamed and moved toward the door.

Grandmother barred her path.

"And do you know what the Gestapo will ask about? The people who hid him. This is a big, smart boy, Panna Monika. He knows your address and your last name."

Grandmother's voice was calm and reasonable.

"Whatever happens to my grandson will happen to you, too," she added for clarity, and put on her coat.

After she left, Monika sat down, put her arms around her belly, and burst into tears. She cried for a long time, out loud, in a thin, wailing voice.

Just in case, you went back into the wardrobe.

In the evening, she called you out. On the table, as every evening, was a frying pan with rosy potatoes fried in lard, and two plates.

Grandma came for you the next day.

You went to a new, strange house.

In it there was a new, strange wardrobe and you were not allowed to go near the windows.

9

I will tell you something.

That girl, the one who was the same age as you and with bleached hair, also knew a lot about the Annunciation.

A policeman in the station house on the Aleje, not far from the railroad station, asked her mother to recite "*Anioł Pański*," "The Angel of the Lord." A blackmailer had brought her there, straight from the train. Her mother had first-class looks and good papers. She was named Emilia Ostrowska; she was the sister of Maria Ostrowska, a Roman Catholic, but she did not know how to pray.

"And you?" the policeman smiled at the little girl. "Will you recite '*Anioł Pański*' for us?"

Naturally, she would recite it. After all, she was a clever little girl with sad eyes.

"The Angel of the Lord visited Our Lady and she conceived through the Holy Spirit. Hail, Mary, full of grace . . ."

"What should I do with you?" The policeman was flustered. He was unshaved, in muddy boots with tall uppers; he yawned after every few words, and probably had been on duty since the previous evening.

"One of them looks like a Jew but knows how to pray, while the other doesn't look like a Jew, but she can't pray. You know what? You figure it out for yourselves, which one is a Jew and which one is a Pole. The Pole will walk out of here, and the Jew will stay. Think it over; you can give me your answer tomorrow."

They spent the night in a cell, on stools, under the dim light of a bare bulb. They discussed it.

"You go," said the mother; "I've lived long enough already."

"You go," said the girl. "They'll catch me, and you have to rescue grandma."

"You have a good sense of people, you'll manage," the mother said.

It was true. That girl could do two things unerringly: recognize decent people and salt red borscht just right.

"I know what we'll do," said the girl. "We'll both stay. Do you see what a splendid idea that is?"

In the morning, the policeman brought in Maria Ostrowska, the one who had tried to find three thousand zlotys for Ruta Muszkatblat.

"My sister a Jewess?!" she shrieked, offended. "Emilka, what are you doing here? I'll have a talk with these gentlemen!"

The three of them walked out of the police station. The mother thought that the policeman trusted Maria's shrieks. Maria believed in the policeman's conscience. Only the girl knew the truth: the Addressee of "*Anioł Pański*" had heard her prayer.

10

You never asked where your grandmother lived, where she was going, or where she got the money for your landladies.

You didn't ask about your mother—you already knew that she wouldn't visit you.

You didn't ask about your uncle Ignacy, your uncle Tadeusz, or your cousin Jaś, so she didn't mention them.

She wouldn't have, even had you asked her.

Not because she considered you a child. She knew you were mature enough to understand.

She didn't tell you because she could not waste her energy.

She was saving you.

It took an enormous amount of strength.

You yourself know how much strength goes into surviving. You must not expend it on words, crying, sadness . . .

So I will tell you about Ignacy, your grandmother's son.

He was Celina S.'s pride and joy.

Tall, raven-haired ("a tall, handsome Jew," as one of his friends described him in a postwar memoir), he got his degree in chemistry and married Irena, a green-eyed blonde with a Semitic nose.

During the war he ran a chemical laboratory for the Popular Guard. He produced incendiary bombs out of materials that could be purchased in stores. They were intended to destroy German grain warehouses and fuel tankers that were headed to the front.

He loved you very much. When they took your mama to the Umschlagplatz, he told his wife, "We will raise him. We will adopt him right after the war."

Three months later, Irena, his wife, on her way home from work noticed a crowd in the street. People were standing there in silence, their heads raised. It took her a while to transfer her gaze to the street lights, from which the bodies of men were dangling. She walked faster. The bodies were still hanging there the next day; she walked past them and went to work. She worked in the Institute of Hygiene. She fed lice—she placed them on skin, they drank blood, typhus vaccinations were made from the blood. When she was on her way home, the wind was howling. The bodies were swinging like gigantic pendulums. This time she walked over to the wall and read the announcement posted on it: "Communists used explosives to blow up the railroad line near Warsaw. For this criminal act fifty communists have been hanged."

Contrary to German custom, their names were not given.

She looked closely at the blue, deformed faces. On one of the lampposts her husband, Ignacy, was hanging—your uncle, the only son of Celina S.

Irena survived. She married and bore two children.

In March 1968, when her son was eighteen years old, she revealed to him that she was a Jew. She traveled to France, underwent cosmetic surgery, and returned with a new nose. Her son was shocked. She had left with a normal Jewish nose, with a slight hook, and came back with a flat, expressionless, Aryan nose. Furthermore, she pretended that nothing had happened, that she had always had such a nose. To the question, Who are you, a Jew or a Pole?, she would reply, "A plant geneticist." She developed new varieties of tomatoes and green peas. In August 1980 she named a pea "Victoria" in honor of Solidarity. It had no taste, like her altered nose, like all these artificially cultivated vegetables.

Every Sunday your grandmother came to their home for dinner. She always brought a Wedel chocolate torte. They weren't available in stores, then; they were purchased at a bazaar, from third parties, for twice the price. Grandma was pleasant, quiet, and very helpful. She was drawn to her former daughter-in-law because memories of Ignacy existed only in her. They did not talk about him. They talked about you, about your playing, about everyday concerns, as one does at family dinners. One Sunday your grandmother took the Wedel torte out of her bag and said, "I don't feel so well." She was feeling cold. Irena brought her a basin of hot water and suggested she soak her feet. Someone said that the water should be cold. A discussion developed about the water. Your grandmother lay down and didn't want to soak her feet. Someone whispered, "She's dying." Irena's son wanted very much to see what death looks like, but they threw him out of the room. An ambulance arrived. Your grandmother died in it, on the way to the hospital. They tried to notify you, but they didn't know where you were. You didn't spend that night at home. You found out the next day. Some other time I'll remind you where you spent that night, although it is one of the few things that you remember very well.

I shall tell you about Jaś, your cousin.

He was the son of a communist, Edward L., and Dorota, a Jew who was a religious fanatic. Dorota was Celina S.'s sister. She converted to Catholicism during the war. She went to church every day, always to the early mass; she took communion and lay prostrate for hours near the main altar. Their Polish nanny, who lived in the countryside, wanted to take Jaś with her, but Dorota wouldn't agree to that. The nanny was a communist; she didn't believe in God, she might have a bad influence on the child. "How could I entrust him to such a woman?" she explained after it was all over, when the boy had been found in his hideout and shot in Pawiak prison with a group of grown men.

Dorota survived. For a while, she lived with you. She continued to attend mass every day and to lie prostrate. She would say, "How fortunate it is that before his arrest Jaś took his First Communion."

I shall tell you about Tadeusz, Celina S.'s nephew.

He was sensitive, with a pretty, delicate face. He got married in the ghetto, to Stefa, a girl from the neighborhood. They lived on Leszno Street. Every night, after curfew the tenants in the apartment house would gather in the courtyard under a tree. They would surround Wajcman the tailor, who knew when the war would end. They listened eagerly. The tailor was an optimist and he knew the end was near. He gave the final date as June. June passed and the war did not end. In July, "relocation to the East" was announced. Wajcman the tailor died in August, together with his wife, his son, and two daughters.

Tadeusz left the ghetto. He found a place to live in the Żoliborz district. Two civilians took him away. A neighbor had denounced him, a woman who owned a grocery store. He was twenty years old.

Stefa survived. She married, had a son, and is a professor of history.

She saw Celina S. for the last time forty years ago. She was sickly. She undid her blouse; she had open, bloody wounds under her breasts. She was suffering from diabetes. She had neither the energy nor the strength for doctors. She had no strength left for anything any more; she wanted to last until the Chopin Competition and hear you play. She missed it by three weeks.

Stefa saw you fourteen years ago. You and she had a conversation in Paris. You had a beard, were animated, and your complexion was unbelievable.

You confessed to her that there were two people in your life whom you couldn't stand. Your grandmother, Celina S., and Dorota, her sister.

11

You survived.

Celina S.'s daughter died, her son died, you survived.

Celina S. reminded you that you have a certain obligation: you have to prove that you are deserving of life.

Celina S. decided that you would become a pianist. A great pianist, of world renown. You had to be great to be deserving of life.

You could not betray your mother, who died in order to improve your chances. You could not betray your murdered family and even, perhaps, your entire people. You were to triumph over fascism. You were to show the world that Jews . . . and so on.

You never studied music. You didn't have time to before the war; you tried to play in the ghetto, but the grown-ups complained that you were getting on their nerves. Despite this, Celina S. believed that you had talent.

You did have talent.

Celina S. decided that you would have the best teacher in the world. At that time, it was Lazare Lévy, a professor in the Paris conservatory.

She brought you to Paris.

Lazare Lévy taught you. He chose you from among three hundred and forty candidates.

In Paris you met your father and numerous West European cousins, uncles, and aunts. They welcomed you emotionally.

"Darling," said one of the aunts to her husband, who was in a wheelchair following a stroke and couldn't hear well. "Look who's come to see us. This is the happiest day of my life since the day our son returned from the war in Spain!"

"Who? Who has come?" the uncle inquired.

"Cousin Celina and her sweet little Andrzejek."

"But you said that they had died," the uncle exclaimed, clearly irritated at her.

"Not at all; they survived, the only ones in the family. Isn't it true that you are very happy?"

"The family . . . ," the uncle muttered. "First they perish, then they're resurrected, you never know what to expect from them."

And encouraged by his son, the hero of the Spanish Civil War, he maneuvered his wheelchair toward the door.

Relations among your family members weren't simple. Your grandmother bore a grudge against your father for not getting you and your mother out of Poland. Your father bore a grudge against your grandmother for distancing him from looking after you. Your grandmother bore a grudge against your father for forgetting about her wartime devotion. And against you because you did not deserve that devotion since you don't resemble Ignacy, her ideal son, her pride and joy. Your father bore a grudge against you for playing gloomy pieces, like Chopin's nocturnes, instead of Liszt's Second Hungarian Rhapsody— and so forth.

You returned to Poland two years later with the deep conviction that the world could happily exist without parents under one condition: that music would exist.

In Poland you were invited to attend a camp for young virtuosos. Your colleagues subjected you to tests. In the morning you received a Bach fugue that you weren't familiar with and which experienced pianists had to study for a couple of days. You played it that evening, from memory, with an extraordinary feeling for its polyphony. Each one of your fingers had a different sound, as if it were a different musical instrument. They didn't believe that you hadn't known that fugue, so they gave you their own new compositions. You sight-read the score, then played it without changing a single note. You overwhelmed them. They looked at you as if you had arrived from outer space.

At age fifteen you decided to join the Union of Polish Composers.

You submitted your application and listed thirteen works: ten études (you added in parentheses: "manuscript in preparation"); ten dances (you added in parentheses: "manuscript lost"); piano sonata ("lost"); Variations on a Theme by Handel ("lost"); Variations on a Theme by Cohen ("in preparation"); Concerto for Piano and Orchestra ("in preparation"). And so on. Only one piece of the thirteen, Suite for Pianos, was neither in preparation nor lost.

On the basis of that one composition you were accepted and recognized as having exceptional talent.

12

In the Union of Composers you met a young, handsome, well-educated man.

"He appeared in my life like a little rabbi," he said about you when I visited him fourteen years later.

"He was a little rabbi," he repeated several times. "He had that special Jewish inner vibration. He also had impeccable taste, absolute pitch, and absolute musicality."

You confessed your love for him.

You drove him to distraction. He was older and felt responsible for you.

You became temperamental and mercurial. You would walk out in the middle of a performance without saying good-bye; you would get up from the dinner table in the middle of a sentence. The next day you would explain that you had had to play the piano immediately. This seemed to him like mere caprice. He couldn't stand capricious behavior, but he reciprocated your feelings. He became your first lover.

One Sunday he stopped you as you were about to leave.

You stayed. You both drank wine and talked about love and music.

Again, you tried to leave.

He said, "Stay; it's still early."

You stayed.

The two of you went to bed.

You returned home the next day. You were surprised that your grandmother wasn't home.

That night you phoned him.

"She died. It's your fault that I wasn't with her. I was punished; I deserved it, because I chose you. I was punished with her death."

You put down the receiver, not listening to his apologies. You didn't want to know him any more.

Many months later the two of you met by accident, on Three Crosses Square, where the building of the Cédib

Beauty School had stood before the war, and where the Planning Commission was constructed after the war.

You walked up to him.

"I have to see you. I can't manage without you."

After a month it turned out that you could manage.

"He met a young violinist," your friend told me. Bitterness dripped from his words, from the dried flowers on the shelves, from the full ashtrays, the medicine vials, and the traveling trunks. The trunks were on the floor in the middle of the living room. Were it not for the dust that had settled on them, one might have thought that they had just been brought in from the entryway. Apparently my host had planned to take a long journey, but had changed his mind.

13

After your grandmother's death you lived alone. The armchair in which she had sat and listened to your playing for hours, half dozing because you practiced most eagerly late at night, was now empty.

The date of the Chopin Competition in which you were supposed to participate was approaching.

You told your professor that you had had a breakdown, and that you were withdrawing from the competition.

People suspected a different reason: you were afraid.

HANNA KRALL

Even then every public appearance terrified you. Before going on stage you experienced an upset stomach; you were paralyzed by stage fright and made mistakes that you never made during a tryout.

So you told your professor.

He replied that by giving up you would be insulting your grandmother's memory. That for her sake you should redouble your efforts and win the Competition.

And so you had one more memory to honor.

Not just your mother, your family, and the Jewish people, but your grandmother, who saved your life.

Your undeniable duty was to redouble your efforts and win.

You did not win. You came in eighth. You received ten thousand zlotys and, as the youngest participant in the Competition, a Calisia piano.

Nonetheless, someone paid attention to you. To be precise, it was Artur Rubinstein, who was present in the audience. He heard something in your playing that the others did not hear. He invited you to the Queen Elizabeth of Belgium Competition that would be held the following year.

14

It was not a young violinist. Your embittered friend was deceived by memory. His place in your life was taken by a green-eyed pianist.

I did not see your lovers when they were young. I know them from novels and I picture them to myself: slender, graceful, golden-haired. Now I observe them at a ball given by the Princess de Guermantes. They have sprinkled their hair with white powder, applied makeup, outlined their lips, veiled their faces with a net of wrinkles. "Time . . . , in order to become visible, seeks out bodies and subjects them to its power wherever it encounters them."

I have a reason to summon Proust. You two were reading him—fortunate ones, not disguised for old age. You brought him back from Paris, returning from Lazare Lévy. You also brought back scores and many recordings.

In Poland at that time people were playing and reading the classics—especially, Russian and Polish classics. Among the French, they read Balzac and Zola because they had unmasked bourgeois society.

You informed your friends that there were others: Proust, Gide, and Camus. You played Ravel for the young pianist, especially his *Gaspard de la Nuit*. You talked about Swann and read *L'Étranger* aloud. He listened to you as if in a drug-induced trance. You parted in the evening; he'd call you at night and since he didn't have a telephone, he'd call from a public booth. The nearest phone was on Constitution Square. Sometimes he would stand there for an hour, in the frost, not feeling the cold.

You longed for a son.

Your colleague at the conservatory was supposed to give birth to him for you. Halina S. was tall, sensitive, nearsighted; she captivated you with her intelligence and girlish charm.

"I become a normal man, a real man with you," you told her, and you went on vacation with her to Czorsztyn. You went out for dinner; right after dinner you were supposed to become a "real man." In the restaurant, a very handsome Bulgarian was seated at the next table. You fell in love with him at first sight and decided to spend the rest of your vacation in Bulgaria. You came back a couple of days later; it was filthy in Bulgaria and you had come down with a stomach flu.

You confessed to the young pianist that you really do still love him, but that you are not in love with him.

"Fine," he replied with severe, manly restraint, because you two had already begun reading Hemingway.

To this day that pianist remembers the number he used to dial every night in the telephone booth on Constitution Square.

He remembers your piano, which had a particular sound, like moving sand flowing through an hourglass.

Ten years later you met again in France.

You said, "I'm sorry, I can't do anything for you," the way one speaks to a demanding newcomer from Poland who expects you to help him.

15

The Queen Elizabeth Competition, one of the most difficult in the world of musical competitions, took place in
May of 1956. You took third place; this time, you did not
betray the memory of your grandmother or of the Jewish
people.

In July you returned to Poland and two months later
you left again, this time for good. One September night
before your departure you proved yourself a "real man"
with Halina S. You were euphoric. You sent a telegram:
"We'll name our son Gaspard." But your joy turned out
to be premature. You gave up sending telegrams and began
writing letters. You wrote about three hundred of them
over the course of twenty-five years. The majority of them
were published in the book, *My Guardian Demon: Letters
of Andrzej Czajkowski and Halina Sander.*[2]

You began with plans: a family, a son, a shared "little
apartment," preferably in Paris, but you soon reconsid-
ered. "Enough of this theater, we have to begin life," you
insisted soberly, and you enthusiastically advised Halina
S. to marry a certain Marek. You wept at the news of
her marriage. You started insisting on a meeting in
Stockholm, but you changed your mind. "We can never

2. Janowska, Anita, ed. *Mój diabet stróż. Listy Andrzeja Czajkowskiego i Haliny
Sander* (Warsaw: PIW, 1988).

meet anywhere," you announced in a sudden feeling of responsibility for Halina S. You both were silent for four years. Then you again began to invite her and withdrew the invitation in confusion.

The two of you met fourteen years after you left Poland. (Halina S. had married in the meantime, had given birth to a daughter, divorced, gotten her doctoral degree, remarried, and been widowed.)[3]

Before her arrival you visited a psychiatrist who knew how to change sexual orientation.

You rented a room for her in a house near yours, with a beautiful garden.

You greeted her arrival at the London Station, full of hope, with a bouquet of roses.

You had changed. You had a beard, were beginning to grow bald, but your hair was still black and wavy, your eyes dark brown (when you were sad or angry, they were slightly crossed), and your teeth were dazzlingly white and even.

You assured her that you were very happy; you brought her home and opened a bottle of wine.

That evening you asked if she had brought sleeping pills. You swallowed three at one gulp and lay down. You woke up the next day around noon. You got up and went to the psychiatrist.

The two of you talked in front of the fireplace, played the piano, listened to records, and thought about the same

3. There is more information about Halina S. in Anita Janowska's book, *Krzyżówka* [Crossword Puzzle] (Wrocław: Siódmioróg, 1996).

thing. You desired it, and you were terrified. Psychiatrists have come up with a description: the anxiety of expectations. The more a person wants something, the more he fears it. Nurses who treat homosexuals know that to decrease fear it is necessary to diminish expectation, but Halina S. was not a nurse.

You got dreamy and told her about the son you two would have. What he was supposed to read, what you would play for him. You would begin with atonal music, then follow it with Bach. "He'll think of Bach as an irritating innovation," you laughed, thinking of the joke you two would play on your son.

You embraced her. You whispered, "We'd be marvelously happy together."

"So let's be together," she answered, and you got angry, because only a man can say such words. A woman is supposed to wait for them, preferably in silence.

She was silent. You were furious that she acted like a dead worm.

She fled after a week.

Then she wrote, and received from you, letters filled with reproaches, explanations, hope, and nonfulfillment.

16

At Rubinstein's request Sol Hurok, America's most famous impresario, took you on.

"Andrzej Czajkowski is one of the best pianists of his generation, and even something greater: he is a miraculous musician," Rubinstein said about you, and Hurok included this sentence in your promotional materials. He introduced one small correction: he changed Andrzej to André, because it was easier to pronounce. You also stopped being Czajkowski. From then on you were Tchaikowsky, like Peter, whom you hadn't valued even before then, and whom from the time of your new Tch, you spoke of with contempt and loathing.

In your official biography Hurok wrote about your grandmother, the hiding places, and your murdered family. Which was all true, but it made you into, in your words, an Anne Frank of the piano.

One of Hurok's people contacted you so he could order tails for you and come to an agreement on terms. Either you were late or you didn't show up for the appointment; as an excuse you said, "As you know, I had a difficult childhood."

Your smile didn't disarm Hurok's representative. He complained about you to his boss, who rebuked you with a fatherly admonition.

You wrote back: "You are right; I should grow up and change. I am changing; I'll start with my name. Czajkowski."

Hurok sent a telegram: "Tchaikowsky or we go our separate ways."

And that was the end of the jokes.

Hurok's ideas got on your nerves.

The Jewish-American ladies who supported artists got on your nerves. They had dyed hair, they adored gold jewelry, they knew everyone, they could do a lot of things, and they twittered about every topic. If the Messiah comes, he will have to come to them because there is no one else, Singer wrote in despair, having in mind precisely those ladies. At the next reception you informed your hostess, who was rich, influential, and very generous, "I am a homosexual, I am attracted to Marxists, I eat with my fingers, I don't bathe, and I support equal rights for Negroes." Despite good reviews you stopped receiving invitations to the United States.

Reasonable admonitions got on your nerves.

Rubinstein and his court got on your nerves, and you let him see it. You should not have been surprised that his maid turned you away at their door, asking you never to come there again.

You treated even the Berlin Philharmonic impolitely when they suggested a concert.

Maybe the world got on your nerves?

I have known people like that. The world got on their nerves—because it existed. It had no right to be after what had taken place, but it existed as if nothing had happened.

17

Józef Kański, a musicologist (you considered him a friend in the conservatory, but you didn't send him a single post-card after you left), told me how you sat at the piano and were afraid to begin.

You were supposed to play Chopin's Nocturne in E♭ Major, which begins with a single protracted note, B♭, after which the melody unfolds.

You sat down, and were afraid to touch the key. You knew how the B♭ should sound, you could hear it, and you panicked, afraid that your hand would not replicate the longed-for sound.

"You play it," you finally said, and Kański touched the key without hesitation.

"You see how easy it is?" he said encouragingly, but you continued to sit there, staring at the keyboard, and listening intently to some inner sound.

Kański says that whether playing other people's works or composing your own, you always knew more than you were capable of expressing. The most beautiful composition, after all, is the work that exists inside oneself. You write it out afterward for instruments, for all those strings, keys, or words, too, and with every note and word that is written down you depart helplessly from the ideal sound.

Your fears overwhelmed you. (Were you afraid that your playing would not meet the expectations of your grand-mother, your mother, your family and people?) The nervous diarrhea returned before every entrance onto the stage.

Before your concert in the Palais de Chaillot you locked yourself in the toilet and could not get out. You finally succeeded in opening the door at the last minute, and wrote about this to the green-eyed pianist, with humor, as befits a description of a most amusing event.

You can't fool me.

I see you in that palace toilet, covered in sweat, trembling, as you struggle with the gilded latch.

It surprises me that you locked yourself in at all.

In New York, at a meeting of Hidden Children—people who were hidden as children during the war—a questionnaire was distributed. One of the first questions was: "Do you lock the door behind you when you go into a toilet?"

I assume that, like the majority of Hidden Children, you did not lock doors; so, what happened in the Palais de Chaillot? Did you lock it because you were distracted?

Tormented by your fear, you played imprecisely. The audience did not notice. You had that magnetic power with which true artists—miraculous musicians, as Artur Rubinstein would say—are endowed.

You played this same composition differently each time—sometimes with feeling, at other times with cold deliberation. You might disrupt the tempo of your playing with rubato in order to draw attention to a fragment that struck you as especially beautiful that day. You communicated not the work but your own spiritual state.

However, is there really an objective truth of a musical composition?

Today, people play differently than in those days: more quickly and without mistakes. It sounds good on compact discs. It is by no means certain that you would have sounded as good. Compact discs don't register the magnetic forces that pulse from the stage.

More about fears . . .

You were tormented by bad dreams.

(That was the next question in the New York questionnaire: "Do you have nightmares? Do you dream that someone is approaching your hiding place and is going to find you at any moment?")

Did someone approach your hiding place? Did you know that the door to the wardrobe would open in a minute and he would notice you, squeezed into a corner, soaked with urine, using the chamber pot to conceal, unsuccessfully, your hair that was growing out dark?

You took sleeping pills. You took too many pills: for sleeping, for waking up, for your nerves, for your stomach, for headaches . . .

From the New York questionnaire:

"Do you get upset about things out of proportion to their significance?"

You worried about everything.

"What do you think, should I start practicing today at eleven or at eleven thirty?" you would ask your friends.

"It's eleven thirty already, and lunch is in an hour. Maybe I should start after lunch?"

"What do you think, should I go at four? Or would six be better?"

And so forth.

18

Occasionally, you would allow yourself to perform wild improvisations.

At the request of the director of a traveling circus whose pianist had fallen ill, wearing a bizarre circus hat on your head you played music that not a single lion or elephant could dance to.

"Can't you see that the animals don't want to dance to your music?" the director screamed, ushering you away from the piano.

"It's because they are listening intently," you replied with dignity as you left the tent.

You agreed to play the Ravel piano concerto in Norway, although you didn't know the music. You had two weeks to learn it. You spent a week with a friend who showed up unexpectedly; at his manager's request you substituted for a sick colleague in the provinces. Only two days were left. You decided to travel by train and learn the notes en route. In your compartment, you reached for your suitcase. You realized that the score was still on your piano.

The director, in despair, greeted you at the station. "A terrible story: the harpist poisoned himself; we can't play the Ravel."

"Mozart," you proposed, resignedly. "Whatever. I play everything."

In fact, you had one concerto "in your fingers" then—the twenty-fifth.

Flipping through scores in the library, you said, "This one's too short, this one's too easy; oh, this is what we'll play!"

You played magnificently. There was a banquet after the concert. You raised a toast to the orchestra, to whom you wished to confess something.

"In the first place," you said, "I have never in my life played the Ravel concerto. In the second place, I remembered only one Mozart concerto, the twenty-fifth. And in the third place . . ." You paused. "It was I who poisoned your harpist."

No one laughed; it's not clear why.

You enjoyed telling your friends similar stories. Despite your dreams and agitation, you liked having a good time. You were "an inexhaustible source of jokes"; people grew accustomed to the quick-witted jester's *emploi*, they idolized "your gambols, your songs, your flashes of merriment, that were wont to set the table on a roar." (These words are about Yorick, the king's jester, but why should I bother mentioning this?—you knew all of *Hamlet* by heart.)

It began to torment you. You complained that you were a monkey who has to put on a show. You confessed to a woman whom you met in South Africa, "On stage and in conversations I acted like an artist and like a clown." (The woman in South Africa has to be, naturally, the daughter of Mrs. Slosberg, who sent you parcels and money after the war. Unfortunately, I don't know her name. There will be no punch line.)

19

From Stefan Askenase, pianist, professor at the Brussels and Bonn conservatories, to David Ferré (recorded on tape):

"I am old, I am almost ninety. I still play and give concerts. Rubinstein played until he was ninety-two.

"I met Andrzej at the Chopin Competition; I was on the jury. He had a marvelous talent and an unusual personality. He became my student. He was not a student who consents to everything, oh no, but he accepted most of my advice. He became more of a friend than a student.

"Will you drink a glass of sherry with me?

"Have you ever heard Andrzej's Inventions? I have a recording of it by the BBC. I also have his Piano Concerto. Radu Lupu performed it in London; it's very lovely.

"A couple of months before his death Andrzej conducted a master class in Mainz. He visited us in Bonn. We spent the whole day together; he took the last train back to Mainz. He didn't feel well in the train; he was in terrible pain. He was operated on the next day. . . . He had bank loans to pay and immediately after the operation he had to perform. He wept into the phone, saying that he would lose his home if he didn't pay off his debts. He played splendidly, but he got sick again. . . . They took him back to England.

"I have the recordings upstairs; please come with me. Oh, here's the Inventions.

"We forgot to take the sherry! Would you go back and get our glasses?

"Someone asked Rubinstein why Czajkowski didn't have a great career. 'Because he didn't work at it,' Rubinstein said. That book of Rubinstein's is good, only there's too much caviar, champagne and crabs in it, and there's not a word about Andrzej. Andrzej once played Prokofiev's Seventh Sonata for Rubinstein seven times in a row. Rubinstein was impressed only by those pieces that he himself had not played.

"Would you believe that I was personally acquainted with Alban Berg? A charming, exquisite man. He fell in love with my first wife. She was very young and very beautiful. When she went to have her hair done before the premiere of *Wozzeck* in Brussels in 1932, Berg waited a whole hour for her. She wrote him a letter afterward:

'Listening to *Wozzeck* I knew which parts you composed when Schönberg was in Vienna, and which you composed during his absence.' That's what she wrote to him; that wife of mine was not shy. He answered her that she had touched upon a matter that was the burden of his life. . . . He was not better than Schönberg, no, but he was different. My friend played his wonderful violin concerto, with Paul Klecki; Klecki was the conductor in Dallas then, but he left a year later. I asked him why. He said that it's impossible to live in a city without sidewalks. In Dallas there wasn't a single sidewalk because everyone rode in cars.

"The greatest composer of the century was Bartók. Naturally, there was also Stravinsky, and others as well, but Bartók is Bartók.

"I heard Andrzej play several of his Inventions in Lisbon. I told him that they were as good as Prokofiev's *Visions Fugitives*. I once heard Prokofiev himself play them.

"I'll play the Inventions for you.

"Wonderful. It's true; not since Bartók has anyone written such a beautiful piece for the piano.

"I'll put on his *Shakespeare Sonnets* for you. They're beautiful, though a trifle monotonous.

"And what about *The Merchant of Venice*? He said that he tried to interest the English Opera in it, but they didn't want it."

And so forth.

I read this with genuine envy.

I wish that you could have spun similar stories at age ninety: a young and beautiful wife, music, a glass of sherry. This is exactly how an elderly artist ought to natter away on a pleasant afternoon.

20

From your diaries:

Jerusalem, 3 December 1980

"I've just woken up from a dream in which . . . I had been handling buried radioactive material. As a result, the skin on my hands was already peeling and I was showing them to the woman concerned (whom I cannot identify). . . . For once I think I can explain the dream. The buried dangerous stuff is my Ghetto past; for the past two weeks I have been delving in it, with increasing horror and revulsion; I've made myself read the Ringelblum Ghetto archives, which appalled me, and Wojdowski's novel on the subject, which I cannot bring myself to continue. I now realize how little I knew, how sheltered I had really been. And how egocentric."

Cumnor, 14 January 1981

"Only now am I experiencing . . . some shadowy sense of kinship with the dead—all of them, not only my mother. They seem that much less dead to me, and I less alive. And now that I see myself as one of them, my fate strikes me as incredibly lucky, almost indecently so, as if I had stolen my survival."

Caracas, 11 February 1981

"(I heard in a dream) a middle-aged German voice (perhaps that of the amiable old German whose daughter let me practise on her piano, and who can be seen both around the house and on a photograph standing on the same piano):

"'Du, da war *noch* etwas!'

"And suddenly, in that split-second before the shock woke me up, I was about to see, I actually caught the first glimpse of what the German had seen . . . : the ovens, the lot.

"I am afraid.

"My first reaction to the dream was to jump out of my bed, drop on my knees and pray to God to preserve my soul. . . .

"I am playing the K.488 here on Sunday, with the first rehearsal tomorrow, so now is just the time to take Valium. . . .

". . . But I am frightened of the 5-day holiday in Miami on the way back. What will befall me there at night, alone with my subconscious in an hotel room? . . .

"BOŻE, BĄDŹ WOLA TWOJA. [LORD, THY WILL BE DONE.]

"I'm afraid."

16 February 1981

"The K.488 went very well yesterday! I love the work and it shows. Somehow the sustained peacefulness of the first movement lends its calm to my own attitude . . . so that I can attend to each detail without haste or panic. I see it as a Madonna, with the Andante as a Pietà. . . ."

21

"I hereby bequeath my body, or any part thereof, to be used for medical purposes in conformity with the regulations of the Law on Human Tissue, and request that the Institution which receives my body should have it cremated afterward, with the exception of my skull, which the Institution is to donate to the Royal Shakespeare Company for use in theatrical performances.

"Signed by the testator in our presence, and then by us in his presence . . ."

You signed it as A. Czajkowski. For the first time since Hurok.

22

Would you like to know how IT is done?

The head is cut off and macerated.

"Macerate" is a professional term used in anatomy. In the nineteenth century the job was entrusted to ants, which are the best at this work. The head was placed in an ants' nest and a week later in the springtime, or four days later in the summer (in the summer ants are more industrious), a skull was removed, clean as clean can be.

Nowadays, after soft tissue like the eyes and lips are removed, the head is heated in a pot of water to no higher than forty degrees Celsius. In order to avoid damaging the delicate bones, among which the most delicate is the lachrymal bone, the head must not be boiled. The lachrymal bone is located near the inner corner of the eye and contains a narrow groove through which the tears flow. Gasoline is used to remove the fat from the bones. Since the synovial capsules and ligaments are destroyed, the jaw is connected to the rest of the skull with fine wire.

That is how it is done in Poland. In the modern world, electric vessels are used. The Warsaw Institute of Legal Anatomy has just received a brochure from a Swiss firm. They are offering a macerator made of nickel-chromium-molybdenum steel, with a two-year guarantee, for one hundred thousand francs. The Institute of Anatomy can't afford that, so you were fortunate that you arranged the matter in England.

Your skull was offered to the Shakespeare theater. First they kept it in the sun so that it would dry out thoroughly and be nicely bleached, and then they performed *Hamlet* with it. After a couple of performances it turned out to be fragile, so they placed it in a carton and put it away in the props warehouse. But before that, they photographed it. Hamlet was holding your skull with both hands, looking into its empty eye sockets. As everyone knows, he was thinking about Yorick, the king's jester, his gibes, his gambols, his songs, his flashes of merriment.

The photograph was enlarged and made into posters.

Do you know that the inmates in a Polish prison wrote and staged a *Hamlet*—in prison argot?

The actor addressed the skull with this monologue:

> I've got a question to put to you, corpse:
> Should one keep dragging on or drop into the grave?
> In short, I have a fear
> that instead of politely smelling the roses
> this harmful soul of mine
> is going to start spilling its sins . . .

You like it, right?

I can see you laughing joyously at the thought of your skull in the hands of a criminal who is serving a fifteen-year sentence. You should have left it to the Division of Prisons in Opole instead of the theater in Stratford.

"Nobody loved that Hamlet, and the dude didn't care about nothing else," the recidivist actor in Opole explained to his fellow prisoners. The perceptiveness and simplicity of this ought to impress you.

The green-eyed pianist said that in the matter of the skull you were being completely yourself: inventive, audacious, filled with art, and yearning to live on in art.

He assumed that you had thought this all up in your youth.

In old age a man begins to think about what comes AFTER and, just in case, prefers to be buried with everything accounted for.

Your body "or any of its parts" was not used for transplants because it was diseased.

Your London girlfriend kept the urn with your ashes in her house for a couple of years.

A while ago she took it to the riverside meadow where your best thoughts used to come to you.

It was a sunny, windy day.

She opened the lid of the urn and waited for the wind to carry off its contents.

23

English became your language. Except for your letters to Halina S., you wrote everything in English. Even your childhood memories, in which your grandmother, Aunt Dorota, your mother, and you appear—you all speak English. Even your diaries.

With the exception of four words in Caracas, written in Polish in block letters in the middle of the page:

BOŻE, BĄDŹ WOLA TWOJA. LORD, THY WILL BE DONE.

You told your psychoanalysts and psychiatrists, in English, about the wardrobe and the Aryan side.

I cannot believe that they understood.

You were walking around with an undiagnosed illness. It is called "survivor's syndrome." In Toronto I witnessed an attempt at curing it—group psychotherapy for a couple of people your age. It was based on narration without an ending, so one woman told about her little brother whom she "had not kept an eye on" in Auschwitz, and the other told about the wardrobe she had tried to enter in the presence of strangers. They had been telling these stories for thirty years, always with terror and weeping.

A year ago the sickness claimed Bogdan Wojdowski, whose book, *Bread for the Departed*, you were reading in Jerusalem. His wife opened the door to his room in order to call him to dinner, and saw him hanging from the window frame. "We both survived, but not completely," Henryk Grynberg wrote after his death. ". . . we paid a price for our survival—a very high price. So high that sooner or later our resources are exhausted."[4]

---

4. Grynberg, Henryk, "Bogdan Wojdowski, My Brother." In *Bread for the Departed*, trans. Madeline G. Levine. Evanston, IL: Northwestern University Press, 1997, p. vii.

24

You also wrote down your conversation with your mother in English.

Apparently, a Polish original existed. It came into being shortly after the war, the day before Mother's Day. Your school assignment was to write an appropriate poem. You had no ideas. Your grandmother was sitting near you, knitting.

She said, "It's simple. Begin with 'Mother, where are you? Why aren't you here?'"

You began, "Mother, where are you? . . ."

You wrote the rest at one go, not lifting your pen from the notebook.

No one knows what happened to the original. I know the version re-created by you, a grown man, thirty years later.

I was afraid to translate it into Polish. I asked Piotr Sommer, a poet and translator of English poetry into Polish, to help me. I wanted to soften the terrible, obscene words, but he wouldn't agree. This is what you screamed at her, and that's how it should remain; these are your words.

This is what you screamed . . .

Even had I not known what you wanted done with your skull, I would have thought that it was a cry of Hamlet's.

Hamlet screams at Gertrude—a son crazed with jealousy and yearning.

Hamlet after Treblinka . . .

"Mother, where are you?"

You wrote the rest in a single breath, without lifting your pen from your notebook.

You knew why she wasn't with you. She had stayed in the ghetto. She had stayed with Albert, her beloved. She preferred to die with him than to survive with you, her son. The poem was a conversation with your mother, so you allowed her to explain herself. "Darling," she said to you, "it was easier to hide a child than a grown woman. I wanted you to be saved. . . ." You started screaming at her. You didn't need her sacrifice. You needed her! You had as much right to death as she had. She deceived you. ("And you lied to me like a slut," you screamed.) You knew, you knew it instantly, that she was lying. She said, "Mummy will be with you in a few days." You knew that she was lying! She begged you to stop screaming. To stop yearning. Your yearning hurts you and it doesn't help her. You exploded in a burst of fury:

> Miss you?
> You fucking sentimental cunt. . . .
> Did you have a nice honeymoon?
> You must have looked a picture, dying in each other's
> arms.

She tried to calm you down: "Men and women died in separate chambers." She assumed that you knew very little about Treblinka. She was mistaken. You knew a great deal! You knew that sometimes the flow of gas was weak, and it took many hours for people to die. You hoped that there had been enough gas for her.

Answer me this.
I am sorry for all I've said. But just answer this!

That's how you talked with your mother.
That's how you screamed!
I think that you were talking with her and screaming throughout your entire life.
Even if she didn't know the arrangements you'd made for your skull, she still would have thought that this was Hamlet's scream.
Hamlet screams at Gertrude—mad with jealousy and a son's yearning.
Hamlet after Treblinka.

The Decision

1

I spent a day with Peter Schok. I didn't like him. This was in Amsterdam; Benjamin G., a translator of Polish literature and a theater director, introduced us. He loved Peter Schok. He said that he had a beautiful, melodious voice. He said that all of him was beautiful, that he was covered with soft, raven-black hair. "Tender violence," Benjamin G. called it in English—a combination of tenderness, masculinity, and strength. This was embarrassing for me, because I liked the previous boy with whom Benjamin G. was still living even though he no longer loved him. I especially liked his photographs. He was particularly fond of photographing interiors without people, with a couple of simple objects: a flower in a vase, peeling paint on a door frame, threadbare tapestry. These things, as is often the case with details, were a metaphor for the eternal questions; they symbolized loneliness and transience.

Peter Schok turned out to be short, pale, and uncommunicative. Everything he wore was black and made of leather. We went out for a walk. He was a Jew, so first he took me to the Portuguese synagogue. He assured me in his melodious voice that it was modeled on the Temple of Solomon and rivaled it in beauty. He came to life in the Jewish museum. He had recently quit his job at a hotel reception desk and accepted a position as a masseur in a sauna, but he looked intently at the portraits of diamond cutters, physicians, publishers, thinkers, and bankers, their wives and children, their rings, tiaras, and strings of pearls, with the pride of someone who was an heir to all of this.

We walked along the canals, which Peter Schok liked; we stopped talking and it became more enjoyable. We drank his favorite wine and ate Indonesian pancakes with seaweed sauce. In the evening he escorted me back to Benjamin G.'s house and said goodbye. He didn't come inside; he didn't want to upset the boy with whom Benjamin G. was still living although he had stopped loving him.

2

"AIDS is a problem for your neighbors," Benjamin G. wrote me in a letter. "At most, you know the people who are dying by sight. But one day someone whose address is in your address book will die. Then someone with whom you once slept. Then someone who is really close to you. . . ."

I have the telephone numbers of some of Benjamin G.'s friends in my address book. They lived in Berlin. Konrad was a pastor and Wolfgang Max Faust, an art critic. I had taken a long walk with the pastor, just as with Peter Schok. For some reason, people who have a life-threatening disease set aside time for me, even though they have so little of it. Perhaps they want to enjoy their world by showing it off? Perhaps they wish to make a gift to other people of the place that is dear to them?

On a hot spring morning, the pastor gave me the gift of the Havel River and the meadows bordering the Havel. We visited the Cecilienhof, where the Potsdam Conference was held (enormous strapping fellows, two meters tall, dressed like soldiers of Frederick the Great's guard, were performing drills in the courtyard), and the nineteenth-century Russian settlement, with little wooden houses that looked like they came from Irkutsk. We were accompanied by the smell of prematurely dried grasses and the steaming river. It turned out that Wolfgang Max Faust, the pastor's friend who had AIDS, recorded each of those days in his journal.

"It was a little too loud," he wrote.

Or, "To do what needs doing and remain without desires."

Or, "Death is an experience of the body. I think about it with my body, not with my head. Everyone should open himself up to welcoming the death within him."

Or, "In art it's no longer a question of art. It's a question of our life. . . ."

And so forth.

He published these notes in a book with the subtitle *The Quotidian. Art. AIDS*, and then he hanged himself in the cellar with a radio cable. Pastor Konrad felt he didn't have the strength to conduct a funeral service. He asked another pastor who was suffering from AIDS to do it. That pastor got permission for the funeral from the hospital. They buried Wolfgang Max Faust in the loveliest Berlin cemetery, not far from Marlene Dietrich.

"If I had to die now, I would say 'Was that all?'," Wolfgang Max Faust observed one day.[1]

Yes, as Benjamin G. predicted, I, too, have people with AIDS in my address book.

A stupid feeling.

---

1. Faust, Wolfgang Max, *Dies alles gibt es also: Alltag, Kunst, AIDS. ein auto-biographischer Bericht.* Stuttgart, 1993.

3

Peter Schok was the next to get sick. He already had a new lover. Benjamin G. explained their breakup to me as Peter Schok's fear of true love. The fear might be the consequence of Peter Schok's Jewish ancestry, Benjamin G. said. The link between his ancestry and his fear was unclear, because Peter Schok was born ten years after the war, and his mother had spent the war years in Great Britain, but this explanation gave the affair the stamp of tragedy and brought Benjamin G. some relief.

The virus settled in his brain. After his surgery, the doctor said the patient had one year to live.

It was January.

Peter Schok visited a woman artist whom he was friends with and asked for a pleasing picture. He selected a lithograph titled *Only So Far, No Farther.*

He looked through volumes of contemporary Dutch poetry. He selected a fragment of a song by Ivo De Vijs: "When I die, come all of you/Be strong or weep, everything will be permitted on that day/All right, let it be crowded and noisy with talk,/On that day I will be in charge of silence."

He listened to several recordings of Jewish songs and also the music from the film *The Rose.*

He ordered an obituary notice from the printer's, such as families send out to their acquaintances to notify them of a death. They are usually decorated with a black frame, but Peter Schok asked to have the cheerful lithograph on the first page. Inside there was to be Ivo de Vijs's song and four words: "Peter Schok died on . . ." and an empty space for the date.

4

In the spring, the premiere of *Le Bourgeois Gentilhomme*, directed by Benjamin G., took place, and although they each had a new partner, Benjamin personally accompanied Peter Schok to the theater.

Peter Schok, already emaciated and weak, sat in his wheelchair repeating, "Look around; everyone is looking at us." Which was true. In Amsterdam, when one man is in a wheelchair and another is pushing him, every passerby looks at them. Everyone knows that it is a gay man pushing his friend who is sick with AIDS.

The performance was very pleasant. It combined Molière's text with the music of Jean-Baptiste Lully, Louis XIV's court composer. The guests sat among the musicians, drank wine, and had the impression that they were guests of the gentleman at a concert in his home. Peter Schok sat in the first row. Black spots, the mark of AIDS, had come out on his feet but had not touched his face. Listening intently in his elegant suit, Peter Schok was beautiful, as in the distant good days.

They had bought the suit in Poland, when he and Benjamin G. were still together. They were on vacation in Zakopane. On the last day they were supposed to go to Kasprowy Wierch, but Peter Schok had returned the hard-won reserved-seat ticket and gone instead to Krupówki, to a jewelry store.

"Why are you doing this? You don't even love her," Benjamin G. marveled, when Peter Schok chose the prettiest string of pearls for his mother.

The next day, they left for Wrocław to see Tadeusz Różewicz's *Death in Old Scenery* and before the performance they bought Peter that suit—elegant, a dark blue with a discreet gray stripe.

During the summer the suit had become so loose that he needed new trousers. They again went by wheelchair and asked for the smallest size in the C&A department store. They were waited on by a nice, sturdy, fifty-ish woman. They loved her. Salespeople usually speak with the man who pushes the wheelchair and avoid looking at the one who is sitting in it, but this woman addressed Peter Schok every time.

In October, Peter Schok and his friend Gerrit asked the doctor what they should expect.

"The end," the doctor answered. "Were you expecting anything else?"

5

Peter Schok named the day: Monday, at 8:00 p.m.

He informed the doctor.

He invited his mother.

Gerrit bought smoked salmon and a bottle of French champagne.

The doctor brought a small bag; the mother, a raven-haired woman with thick eyeglasses and the string of Zakopane pearls on her short neck, brought a bouquet of flowers.

Peter was sitting in an ordinary armchair, with a blanket on his knees.

They ate the salmon, drank the champagne, listened to Beethoven's *Eroica* Symphony. When the music stopped, the doctor turned to Peter Schok.

"Do you know what we are going to do now?"

"I know," Peter Schok replied.

"Is this what you want?"

"Yes."

This was an official conversation in conformity with the Dutch law about "medical decisions concerning the termination of life." The disease was incurable. The patient had expressed his wish. Those present were witnesses. On the following day the doctor would have to file an appropriate report in court. The essential conditions had been fulfilled.

The doctor removed a bottle from his bag and filled a glass with a clear, bright yellow liquid. Peter drank half of it.

"I don't want this," he said. "Please give me an injection."

He had been afraid of injections throughout his life, but now he rolled up his sleeves and spoke calmly to the doctor.

He died in his sleep five minutes later.

Gerrit, a nurse at an old-age home, carried the corpse to the bed. He washed it with professional skill and dressed it in the Wrocław suit.

The funeral home supplied the coffin that Peter had selected and ordered. It had a glass lid and a cooling system concealed under its floor.

His friends came together, alerted by Gerrit's sending out the colorful obituary notice. Most of them were infected with the HIV virus. They laid down flowers and lit candles. Synagogue music flowed from tapes. Peter Schok's little red cat came up to the coffin and stared at him through the glass lid, astonished by the sight. That was the only detail not foreseen by Peter in the program of his funeral celebration. His friends chased the cat away, but it climbed up again. After consulting briefly, they agreed that it wasn't hurting anything and they allowed it to stay.

The crematorium is located outside the city, not far from the sea.

Again they listened to Jewish songs, and then the music from the film *The Rose* rang out. It was sung by Bette Midler, the New York actress who began her career in gay men's bathhouses; they were the first to hear her songs.

As she sang "And you think that love is only for the lucky and the strong," the floor, with the catafalque and coffin, began to descend, like a trapdoor in a theater. The music ceased. The program prepared by Peter Schok was over.

In the silence, and not included in the program, the empty floor returned to its place.

6

Beside the Prinsengracht canal, not far from the church whose bell Anne Frank could hear in her hiding place, there stands or, rather, lies, a monument. It is composed of three pink triangles; that is how homosexuals were labeled in the German camps. The triangles descend lower and lower in the direction of the canal; the last one is immersed in the water. There is a plaque on it with the inscription, "To the memory of the homosexuals who were persecuted during the Second World War, before then, afterward, and whenever." Every so often, unknown perpetrators tear off the plaque, but gays replace it with a new one. To the question, What connection is there between AIDS and the camps and the war?, they reply that it is discrimination and hatred.

After they returned from the funeral, Peter Schok's friends placed flowers next to the plaque, which was in its proper place that day.

Dutch regulations require the burial of ashes immediately after cremation. They are sprinkled in the crematorium garden or placed in a collective tomb filled with urns, known as a columbarium, which in Latin means a dovecote. Recently, permission has been given to keep ashes at home. Gerrit took advantage of the new law, brought Peter Schok's ashes home, and put them in his wardrobe. He asked his friends to mix their ashes, his and Peter's, and to bury them together when his turn comes, and it will not be long in coming.

7

Benjamin G. asked Peter Schok's mother why Kaddish wasn't said at the funeral.

"What's that?" his mother asked.

"The Jewish prayer for the dead."

She was taken aback.

"They should have said Jewish prayers for my son?"

It turns out that Peter Schok was not a Jew.

His mother tried to understand why her son wanted to be seen as a Jew, but Benjamin G. didn't know either. Did he wish to abase himself? Did he wish to elevate himself? Was he trying to enroll in the world that he had looked at with such admiration in the Jewish museum?

8

People who are suffering from AIDS are different and they want to die in a different way. They create liturgies of disappearance. They believe that they will become familiar with death and that they won't be afraid.

Peter Schok ended the scenario with a request for euthanasia. He believed that he had found an appropriate, simple, tasteful form. He was mistaken. It turned into kitsch, because the form was false. It created the illusion that Peter Schok was deciding about his death. In reality, the decision had already been made, but not by him. Peter Schok only chose the date, the music, and the menu.

Nonetheless, one cannot deny Peter Schok's courage.